Praise for *HEALING GRIEF*. . .

"Not since *Gilgamesh* have we had such a detailed map of the bewilder-
ing territory of grief. Rosalie Deer Heart's gift is the assurance that we
need never again go this way alone."

Alfred DePew
Author of *The Melancholy of Departure*

"*Healing Grief* is an inspiring story of 'unseen connections' that bridge
life and death, of multidimensional perspectives that allow us to grieve
our loss and shed old skins in order to embrace the essentials of life's
purpose. It compels us to awaken to our aliveness and our innocence.
Rosalie Deer Heart has written one woman's journey toward wholeness
which is truly that of every woman."

Sheryle Baker, MA
Executive Director, The LIFE Center
Tampa, Florida

"Rosalie Deer Heart has an angel in her journal. Her documentation of a
mother's grief and the simultaneous awakening of her psychic powers
under the tutelage of her son's spirit makes for compelling and hope-
filled reading. This is the spiritual journey written from its raw and open
heart."

Christina Baldwin
Author of *Life's Companion: Journal Writing As a Spiritual Quest*
and *Calling the Circle: The First and Future Culture*

HEALING GRIEF
A Mother's Story

ROSALIE DEER HEART

Foreword by Joan Chadbourne, EdD

Heart Link Publications
San Cristobal, New Mexico

Published by: **Heart Link Publications**
PO Box 273
San Cristobal, NM 87564

Edited by Ellen Kleiner
Book design by Richard Harris
Cover design by Janice St. Marie
Front cover photo by Rosalie Deer Heart
Back cover photo by Meredith Jordan
Logo by Marianna Lands

Printed in the United States of America

Publisher's Cataloging-in-Publication Data
Heart, Rosalie Deer.
    Healing grief : a mother's story / Rosalie Deer Heart ; foreword
by Joan Chadbourne.
    p. cm.
    Includes bibliographical references.
    ISBN 0-9651576-0-1

    1. Heart, Rosalie Deer. 2. Grief--Case histories. 3. Parenting
--Psychological aspects. 4. Bereavement--Psychological aspects.
I. Title.

BF575.G7H43 1996   152.4
                                          QBI96-20213

10 9 8 7 6 5 4 3 2 1

In Gratitude

Deepest appreciation to Michael Bradford, who provided the finances to publish this book and took on the challenge of teaching me about personal love; to Audrey McGinnis, my spiritual mother, who reminded me gently and often that spirit was "growing me up"; and to Bob Eberle, who resides in spirit, for his confidence in me as a teacher, friend, and coauthor.

Special acknowledgment for the love and support of Alison Strickland, Maggie McClain, Louise Zubrod, Susan Lindsay, Mary Elizabeth Mason, Maryrae Means, Christinea Johnson, Anne Campbell, Anne Hubler, John Hornecker, Gary Race, Phillip Levine, and Rendle Leatham. I honor each one as a cheerleader of my soul.

Ellen Kleiner, my editor, who lived in my heart as she did her "word magic" in editing this book, deserves an angel award.

Finally, gratitude to my parents for creating the opportunity for me to do my earth walk.

This book is dedicated to:

My son, Mike Hall, who taught me how to bridge dimensions,

My grandfather, Linwood Jellerson, who lived a multi-dimensional life,

My grandmother, Shirley Jellerson, who has loved me unconditionally since the beginning of time,

My daughter, Kelli-Lynne, who has inspired me to practice unconditional loving, and

Children of the future who bring healing to their families and our planet.

Contents

Foreword

ROSALIE DEER HEART IS MY TEACHER. Her mentor is life itself, the details of which are poignantly recounted in these pages.

The events recorded here took place almost twenty years ago, when she was struggling with the death of her son. As a result of her willingness to surrender to grief, she has become a soul healer—an interpreter and guide linking those who reside in the world of the living with those who dwell in the land of spirit. With her assistance, dying and grieving become imbued not only with sadness and loss but with joy, beauty, intimacy, and deep love. These are the fruits of her journey.

Although Rosie and I have worked together for several years, I had not tasted of these particular fruits until this past summer, the last months of my mother's life. In June my mother, Rose Warrington, was bedridden after surgery to remove a cancerous brain tumor. The operation had rendered her unable to move or talk for two weeks. The rudiments of movement and speech began to return when Rosie made her first visit.

She walked into the room, and Mom—who had little strength in her vocal chords and had spoken only a few words since the surgery— looked up and said, "I saw you last night." Although the two had never met other than in Mom's dream, her face brightened with the spark of recognition.

Rosie joined her energy with Mother's and eventually explained: "You are pretty confused. You are seeing the light of people's souls and not their physical forms. You didn't think you could do this while you were still in your body, did you?" After a long pause, a look of comprehension and relief filled Mom's face, and she whispered, "No."

Rosie returned for weekly sessions, some of which were spent in apparent silence. She seemed able to help Mom focus and concentrate enough energy to articulate her thoughts. One day, after a long period of silence, Rosie noted that Mom wanted something, and asked her to voice her request. Mom looked me directly in the eye and said, "I want to be part of your life." Years, maybe lifetimes, of protective separateness melted with those magical words. Every cell of my being reverberated with love and being loved.

One morning in late July, Mother woke up speaking of "the baby." Rosie came that day, connected with Mom, and helped me understand what was occurring. The day before, it turns out, would have been the forty-ninth birthday of Mom's stillborn child named Deborah. When I asked Mom if this is who she was referring to, she affirmed with a smile that yes, she had been with Baby Deborah during her sleep.

Later in the session, Rosie helped Mom begin to let go. She apparently traveled far out of her body, and Baby Deborah seemed to be guiding her. Mom told us they were searching for her "resting place." The pilgrimage continued on into the afternoon. All the while, people came to visit and were able to feel the serenity that filled the room. At one point Mom, with a faraway, open-eyed expression on her face, said softly, "It is so beautiful."

A few days later, eight of us were at Mother's bedside singing, massaging her, praying, and crying. Suddenly she opened her eyes and looked directly into mine. I reminded her, as I had before, "I want you in my life." Then she closed her eyes, took her last breath, and died.

Rosie came to help the family mourn and celebrate. She continues to guide the connection between Mother and me. I am convinced that because of Rosie's willingness to expand nearly twenty years ago, two souls laboring as mother and daughter have, in recent months, come to recognize each other's beauty and surrender to their mutual love.

Healing Grief, Rosie's story, was a source of comfort for me as my mother lay dying, and it nourishes me even now, as the grieving process continues. It is a life-and-death story certain to soothe and inspire all who come to it.

Joan Chadbourne, EdD
Portland, Maine
January 30, 1996

Introduction

$\mathcal{A}$lmost two decades have passed since the sudden death of my son, Mike. I had just turned thirty-three years old, and he was soon to be fifteen. Weeks before his death, I had agreed to an unwanted emergency hysterectomy, and he had enjoyed his first date. Together we had weathered the painful individuation process that seems to turn mother and teenager into adversaries. And I was delighted when Mike returned to his witty, assertive self, able to be comfortable with the family and even reaching out to his two-and-a-half-year-old sister, Kelli-Lynne.

Then he was dead, and I had no clue how to make the pain go away. None of my friends in our small town in Maine had lost a child. Neither my parents nor my grandparents had ever experienced the death of an offspring. The place in which I voiced my agony, questions, and terror that my daughter, too, would die was my journal. There I kept track of my dreams as well. Indeed, one of the few parts of my life that survived the death of my son was this dedication to writing. Not only did my voice on paper keep me honest rather than held hostage to denial; it helped me maintain my sanity during many years of trying to make sense of my life and my son's death.

My intent was never to write a book. I was simply writing in my journal, as I had since the age of twenty-five. A private person, I had been

1

well trained by a conservative Maine family to keep my feelings and vulnerability to myself, and hence locked away in private journals. As time progressed, however, I surrendered to an unfamiliar way of knowing—a soul imperative, you might say. From then on, my writing and my life felt guided. And I played my part by dutifully recording the day-to-day details of the grieving and healing process that was to claim me for nearly seven years, and that presented many inexplicable interventions for which I had no name and little advance preparation.

Had I known nearly two decades ago what I know now, I would have shouted and allowed my raw emotions to rip through my body; cried openly and told my story repeatedly to family members, friends, even strangers; adapted less to the expectations of others and more to my own unpredictable feelings; been more patient with myself and others; invested in ongoing therapy with a grief specialist; joined a support group for grieving parents rather than looking for answers in books; shared my night dreams and unseen experiences of Mike with people close to me; taken more time for myself without feeling guilty; and loved myself and my daughter more. Instead, I grieved silently and wrote feverishly.

Years later I began reading portions of my journal to other parents who had survived the sudden death of a child. I met with mothers and fathers in Maine, New York, Florida, New Mexico, Colorado, California, England, Scotland, Egypt, and Bali. Each time I shared parts of my story, parents cried. And I felt the pain of grief once again, as well as the transformation that accompanies the sharing of a tragedy.

It has since become clear that I made a soul agreement with my son to record and publish this journal, which I fondly refer to as "Mike's book." Death, I now know, is a teacher. And this book is a work of love and service. My son's death, as well as his life, was my inspiration. I pray that you, dear reader, also discover hope and meaning in your journey through grief to healing.

Today my world is ended.
My heart no longer sings.
I fold my pride about me
As angels fold their wings.
　　　　　—Pearl S. Buck

Year One

March 30, 1977

I have not been able to write anything this past week. Yet, I must keep track of myself in my journal so I will not slip away.

"I'm terribly sorry. There was nothing we could do. Your son is dead."

"Impossible!" I said. "There must be some mistake."

Only an hour before, Mike and his best friend, Artie B., had darted out of the house to shovel snow. I had promised to reward them with a blueberry pie when they returned. My last words to them were, "Be careful." Both boys made faces at me as they bounded into the snow.

"Ma'am, are you okay?" someone in a white coat asked me.

I had thought Mike had broken his leg or arm when the men from the rescue truck first rushed me to the hospital. We had stopped next door to leave Kelli-Lynne with my neighbor. The driver told me nothing during our five-minute ride, so I assumed he knew nothing. When we pulled into the emergency entrance, a television cameraman recorded our arrival. I waited alone for who knows how many minutes in a private waiting room, knowing nothing while everyone around me was aware that my son was dead on arrival. I felt like I was watching a bad movie.

Then I was ushered into a small examining room. All I could ask was, "Did he suffer?"

"No, ma'am, he was electrocuted. He died instantly."

A priest and two nurses appeared, as if on cue. The nurses hovered around me. I was relieved to know Mike hadn't suffered. But he was dead and had died alone. Without me. In the school yard right next door. Why hadn't I looked out the window? Why hadn't I seen the first rescue truck? Would I have been able to save him? We had spoken earlier about the downed power line. Mike and Artie B. had been in the kitchen when I called the power company to report the dangerous wires, and they heard me speak to several neighbors about the potential hazard.

The priest reached out to me, and I collapsed into his arms, crying. Somewhere, somehow I found the words to ask him to say a prayer for Mike, even though we were not Catholic. Looking up, I noticed the nurses fumbling with their hands, and the faces of strangers peering through the window of the cubicle.

I felt utterly alone, in spite of the priest and three nurses crowded in the tiny examining room with me. I could not force myself to believe that my son was dead and I was alive. Without warning, spasms convulsed through my chest, leaving me breathless. I was seized by the urge to run away, hoping that if I ran, I would wake up and realize this was a vivid nightmare and Mike was alive. Nothing made sense to me. Hospitals, I thought, are supposed to be places of healing, not of death.

At that instant my husband, Gil, appeared. I watched as the doctor greeted him. I tried to join them, but my feet wouldn't budge. Although I couldn't hear the words, I saw the doctor's mouth and head moving, then Gil opened his mouth. His face turned pale.

Someone ushered us into a small anteroom. Gil sobbed, saying that every father has high hopes for his son, and now . . . The rest of his words were drowned out by the sounds of my sobs. Then, in a voice I did not recognize as my own, I demanded to see Mike. A nurse replied, "His body is only two rooms away."

"His body!" I screamed. "No, you don't understand. I need to be with my *son,* not his *body.*" I needed to make sure no pain was visible in Mike's eyes. Gil asked the nurse if seeing him was a good idea. I didn't wait for an answer. I was on my way to my son.

I walked unsteadily into the large room. I shuddered when I saw Mike on the operating table. He was so still. For a few moments I reassured myself, remembering how he had looked after an eye operation at the age of four. He is simply resting, I told myself. Naturally he is pale. His eyes are glazed because of the anesthesia.

When I moved closer to touch his arm, I winced as if I had been burned. His arm was cold, plasterlike. And he did not move. I scanned his body for blood. Unable to find any, I knew he had to be alive. Everyone had been mistaken: this was a bad dream, and we would all wake up. Then I touched his face; it, too, was cold. And from somewhere deep inside myself I realized that Mike's body wasn't Mike anymore.

A doctor arrived, motioned me into the hallway, and explained that they had "worked on" Mike, even though he was dead on arrival. Brain damage was irreversible. If Mike had responded to the life-support machinery, he would have been a "vegetable." I looked at the doctor while he spoke, but I had nothing to say. Words had lost their meaning.

As Gil wandered off to speak to a man about funeral arrangements, I pushed my way back into "Mike's room" and demanded to be left alone with my son. I had an inner imperative to do something that mattered although I had no idea what that might be. Standing by myself in the operating room, I was startled by the unexpected presence of Mike's energy. He was no longer a teenager but rather a stream of energy. Part of my mind had become like a beam operating with built-in radar to track this energy. With stunning clarity, I somehow registered that Mike was disoriented, and I rushed in with questions.

"Why? Why? How could you have done this? How could you have been so stupid?" Screaming, I added, "How could you have left me like this?" I felt an overwhelming urge to blame him, guilty that I hadn't been there to keep him alive, and disheartened that I had never taken a cardiopulmonary resuscitation course.

Suddenly the aspect of myself that instinctively tracked energy reemerged, and I perceived that Mike knew nothing about his death. He did not realize what had happened or where he was or what this was all about. I realized I was not being helpful.

A wave of unconditional love for him extended outward from my heart, and I whispered, "Okay, Mike. You did whatever you did. Now you are confused, and I am not helping you with my questions and my anger. Clinging to your physical body is no longer appropriate. Your vibrations are of a different nature. Your energy does not belong here anymore. You must continue on your way. You must leave—now."

Leaning over, I kissed his unmoving lips. Then, with all the energy I could muster, I gave him a swift mental kick to assist him in "moving on." I sighed deeply and then inhaled in spurts, tears welling from my eyes.

"Leave," I told him. "Don't waste your energy by trying to comfort us. I release you. I, who mothered you, release you."

I wiped the tears from my eyes, astounded that from somewhere deep within me I had known what to say. The knowing felt ancient. Yet, I wondered, if I was doing this right, why did my heart convulse? Who was this person intent on ordering her only son out of her life?

The door opened, and two nurses came in. They gave me a tranquilizer. The door opened again, revealing Gil and a priest. The priest told us that the story of Mike's death would be broadcast on the six o'clock news. He gently advised me to call family members at once. Woodenly, I dialed my parents' number, not knowing what I would say and half wishing no one would answer.

Mom picked up the phone. I sobbed, "Oh, Mom, Mom. Mike had an accident, and we are at the hospital, and he is dead." I heard my mother scream. The sounds of her anguish reminded me of my own, and sobs drowned my voice. Gil took the telephone and spoke to my father. I heard him say, "We're doing as well as can be expected." The words sounded singsongy, and I had no idea what they meant. We did not have time to call other relatives before the depersonalized television broadcast. Unable to figure out what I was thinking or feeling, but aware that I was tired of being looked at, I told Gil I wanted to leave.

In the car, I struggled between wanting to go home and wanting to be with Mike. "I have been a mother for almost fifteen years," I said aloud, squirming in the seat to make myself small. If I were little, I thought, I'd be able to diminish the impact of my son's death. Yet, the cold evening air itself felt filled with death.

"We're going home now," Gil said without emotion.

"Home," I echoed. The word no longer had meaning for me. "What's a home without a whole family?"

How I wished we had sold our house in January, as planned. If we had moved, Mike would still be alive. Children are supposed to outlive their parents. Doctors are supposed to heal people. Assumptions passed through my mind like fireworks. Nothing and everything mattered all at once.

Walking in the front door, I was greeted by three eight-by-ten-inch photographs of Mike that he had placed carefully on the mantle two weeks ago, saying brusquely, "so you will see me everywhere." Had he known about his fate? There was no time to torture myself with a parade of "what ifs," however, because our neighbors had heard the news and been on the lookout for our return.

Artie B.'s parents were the first to arrive. "How is Artie B.?" I asked, trembling. He had been at the scene of Mike's death and, as I already knew, had not been hurt. "He is alive," said his mother. I wanted to ask more questions about how he was really doing, but I had no energy.

People appeared and sat quietly in our living room. Everyone's face was pale. Then my mother and father arrived, followed by my brother and sister-in-law. I cried by myself in a corner, not wanting to tell the story of my son's death. Mom sat beside me, urging me to be strong each time tears spilled from my eyes. The telephone sounded like an endless record, even though my brother was fielding the calls.

How rapidly word had spread! Even our best friends had come. They offered to babysit for Kelli-Lynne. Neighbors invited relatives to stay with them. People were being outgoing and generous. I, on the other hand, was in a fog. The only reality I registered was the soreness I had created by clutching and rubbing my hands together.

Decisions had to be made. What kind of funeral will there be? Flowers? The obituary? Should Kelli-Lynne attend the funeral? How does one tell a two-and-a-half-year-old child that her big brother is dead? What do we do with his body? What clothes do we bury him in? Bury? What are our choices? Choices? He's dead. There *are* no choices.

At nine o'clock, the house was suddenly empty. I walked next door to pick up Kelli-Lynne. As she was almost asleep, we decided to tell her about her brother in the morning. I hugged her too tightly. She wriggled free and told me I was hurting her. We tucked her into bed. Quietness settled upon us. Gil and I were alone, and life as we had known it was gone—was dead, like Mike. I was numb, fractured, and embarrassed. I avoided looking at Gil. I had nothing to say and felt sentenced to silence.

During the night, I slept some, and in between I awakened myself with crying or shaking, sometimes both. While awake, I'd force myself to remember that I would not hear the usual morning clamor of Mike's size-twelve boots, or the clattering of dishes in the kitchen, or the never-ending opening and closing of the refrigerator door. There would be no last-minute phone calls from Artie B., no cracking teenage voices drifting through the house from the three boys who walked to school with Mike each weekday.

As always, morning came. Surrounded by silence, I looked out our bedroom window to see the gang, minus Mike, walking by.

I heard Kelli-Lynne whimper, and realized I had to tell her before family and friends came. Sobs from the bathroom interrupted my thoughts. Kelli-Lynne asked why her dad was sad. Now is the time, I prompted myself. In a quiet voice, I asked Kelli-Lynne to sit beside me. She began to chatter about her evening, but time was running out, so I pressed on.

"Kelli-Lynne, brother was hurt very badly when he touched a wire. The doctors at the hospital could not fix him. Medicine could not help him. He is dead. That means we will never see him again."

I took a giant breath and waited. Kelli-Lynne stared at me. I started to cry, and she said, "Don't cry, Mommy, or you will choke."

Where did she hear that? I wondered. She looked puzzled, then asked, "Am *I* your son now?"

"No, Kelli-Lynne. You will always be our daughter."

"Is Mikey still my brother, even though he is dead? Am I still his sister?"

Nobody had prepared me for her questions, just as nobody had prepared me for Mike's death. Or for that matter, life itself.

"Yes. You are still brother and sister, but Mike does not live on this earth or in this house anymore."

"Oh. Now can I play?"

I was disappointed and confused by her reaction. I wanted her to feel the same way I did. I wanted to be able to hold her. But all she wanted was to play!

I went through the motions of straightening up the house before people arrived. Then Gil handed me the newspaper and insisted that I read the obituary and the story of Mike's death. In the obituary I was glad to see that "the family" was requesting, in lieu of flowers, contributions to a scholarship fund we had set up for this year's top all-around student athlete. But reading about Mike's death did not lift me out of the fog. Who cares about the facts? I asked myself. He is dead, and facts will not change anything.

Family members arrived again. Then everyone started talking at once, suggesting the proper way for me to grieve: "Take a tranquilizer," "Be strong," "Cry, and get it all out," "Don't cry," "Let someone else handle the details," "Be sure to make all the arrangements."

At first, I wanted everyone to be quiet. Although their words all made sense and I knew they were well meaning, I felt strangely empty, and their conversations were not filling me up. Then I wished they would talk to distract me. I fantasized that if everyone continued to talk, we could forget the appointment at the funeral home. I could tell the undertaker, "I'm sorry, but I couldn't leave with all those people at my house." I even imagined myself saying, "I'll come another day, when I don't have company."

After a while Gil and I went to the showroom of the funeral home. It was packed with empty caskets—some opened, some closed. The burial-versus-cremation decision was no problem. A few years ago, Mike and I had signed living wills and had expressed a desire to be cremated, which caused a furor in the family. The night before, Gil and I had decided to abide by Mike's decision, against the wishes of both our families.

The casket decision was a major problem. Why bother buying a casket that will only be burned? At first I fantasized about renting a coffin. Then I tried to imagine which coffin Mike would have chosen. Then I felt crazy. The irony of trying to choose a casket Mike would have liked caused me to giggle. Abruptly, tears choked my giggles. This was not a play I had a role in—it was real life, I told myself. But what about Mike's life? I clenched my jaw tighter to avoid screaming, pointed to a solid oak box, and it was done.

The minister arrived and asked if we had any preferences for the funeral service. Part of me took offense at this entire process. Who is a funeral home "home" to? How can a funeral be a "service"? What if I don't want one? Our *lives* are supposed to be a service, not our *deaths*. Another part of me had some ideas. I told the minister I wanted a nondenominational service assisted by a Protestant minister and a close friend named Michael Dwinell, an Episcopal priest. I insisted that the service focus on letting go, hope, and healing.

Leaving the stale, piped-in air of the coffin salesroom, Gil and I decided to walk along the neighborhood beach before returning to our overpopulated house. As we stepped onto the sand, I stopped short, for I noticed out of the corner of my eye a downed wire. If the wire were live and I ran over and touched it, I would be dead in seconds, I reasoned. My instincts propelled me to touch it, for then I could be with

∞ ∞

Mike; I could see him, hold him, even punish him for being so stupid. Struggling to be sensible, I took a breath of cold air and decided to walk on the beach as planned.

This beach used to be our playground. Here Mike and I had gone swimming, scavenged for sea glass, watched hundreds of lobster boats. One day he even launched his own small boat here. I loved to watch him give his sister piggyback rides in the sand; sometimes he would slip, and they would both topple to the ground.

Suddenly, I started to run. I kept moving, hoping that if I ran till I was out of breath, I would feel something other than pain. My breath stretched out in front of me, white wisps of life, but the pain did not go away. I wanted to run forever. Within minutes, however, I fell to the ground, exhausted. More than anything, I wanted someone to hold me—to assure me that Mike was all right, that we would survive, that I had been a good mother, and that I was not being punished by Mike's death. I wanted this fairy tale person to smooth my hair, and to not expect me to do or say or feel a thing. Most of all, I wanted this someone to tell me why my son had died. But no one came. I remained alone and cold.

When we got home, I caught snatches of conversations, hoping to hear a magical phrase that would erase the pain, but no one present had lived through the death of a teenager. Turning inward, I plagued myself with questions. What if we had bought that other house? What if the power company had cut off the electricity when I had called earlier in the day? What if someone had been outside to warn Mike not to go near that wire? Or what if his death was inevitable and could not have been prevented? People looked at me, not knowing that I was torturing myself. I remained quiet and polite, all the while feeling as if my heart wanted to vomit.

Then someone gave me a package wrapped in brown paper. I tore it open, glad to be doing something with my hands. It was a game I had ordered for Mike, a game called Life. "Is there a game called Death?" I heard my monotone voice say out loud to nobody in particular. Turning to a friend sitting nearby, I asked, "Who has the rule book?"

"For what?" she replied.

"Death," I said simply. "Or Life—they feel the same to me."

My friend looked confused. Quietly, she reached over and squeezed my hand. I swallowed hard, ordering my tears not to spill over. I had to take charge of the game called Life. Obviously, I could do nothing about the one known as Death.

I felt disoriented as I drifted in and out of conversations. On all sides of me people were telling Mike's story. I listened as they shared their memories. From time to time, my eyes circled the crowded living room and zeroed in on Mike's winter jacket, then two bags from the hospital marked "Patient's Belongings," then the three school pictures on the mantle.

By midafternoon, I was numb. My lips moved, I hugged people back, and I drank whatever was put in front of me. I felt like a puppet. At one point I overheard someone whisper that I was in shock.

After Gil's family arrived I heard my brother-in-law say, "Losing a son must be more difficult than losing a spouse."

Losing? I wondered. Losing means there is hope of finding. *Death is not losing.*

My brother came. He confided that he had just been at the funeral home, where he'd had a long talk with Mike. He swore at him, then put his silver fish ring on Mike's finger because Mike had been the fisherman in the family. I flashed onto my thirty-third birthday party, which Mike had hosted only three weeks ago, serving up some fish he had hooked while ice fishing. I felt like a dead thirty-three-year-old mother.

At precisely seven o'clock that evening, hundreds of people gathered at the funeral home for the wake. Friends who once were married and were now divorced arrived together. People who were present in my life when Mike was born were present once again. Scores of Mike's friends and classmates came, and teachers mingled with their students. We were all connected to one another through Mike, who lay silent and still. People spoke of their memories of him, and of their sadness. Those who hadn't seen each other in years clustered together, and I watched their reunions with envy. I remember thinking, Mike would have been so grouchy if he had to be here. He hated crowds and resisted being fussed over.

I walked cautiously into the waiting room, where I recognized several of Mike's classmates. They looked grown-up and awkward in their dress clothes. "Thank you for coming," I said to them. "I know this must be hard for you." Motioning to the casket, I asked quietly if they had seen Mike.

One of the boys whispered, "We don't know how to do it. We don't know how to look at him."

I nodded and I invited them to follow me so they could begin to deal with his death. "Mike would have wanted this," I whispered to myself. It

∞ ∞

was all I could do for him. Still I thought, If only I could be Peter Pan, leading these kids on an exciting adventure instead of to a casket.

For two hours, faces swirled before me. Masses of people filled the three rooms. I felt our communion. With so many friends and family members gathered, I thought, we should be celebrating a birth, a marriage. Then I remembered why we were all here. I felt cast in the double role of hostess and grieving mother. Embraces slowed me down; words were hollow; silence was a relief. I moved in search of the silence.

At last my father took my hand and told me visiting hours were over. Only then did I notice that most of the people had left, and with them the heavily scented "flower forest" that had infused the air. No wonder I had requested no flowers, I told myself. I love them, but not now, not this way. Only the spindly cactus fern at the end of the coffin was appropriate. Mike had bought it for me because, as he said, "It was so ugly no one else would buy it."

That night I fell into bed without bothering to undress. But I could not sleep. My mind kept re-creating the day of Mike's death, trying to pinpoint an answer. At two-thirty in the morning I asked for a sign that Mike was okay. Instantly, a huge white dove filled the bedroom with its blinding light. The coming of the dove relieved the ache in my heart, but not the doubt in my head. Did I create the dove? my mind wanted to know.

No sooner had I posed the question than a large, mangy black crow raucously announced itself. I recognized this bird. Only last summer Mike had tripped over a crow with an injured wing and adopted him. He was a bother, but Mike loved him. Despite Mike's devotion, the crow died . . . and now it was flying around my bedroom. My head and heart merged in believing this sign. Only Mike would have had the sense of humor needed to manifest this mangy crow as his emissary.

As the clock ticked on, I came to understand that Mike was engaged in a process I knew nothing about. And I began to wonder if asking for a sign would always work. Who is in charge of all this? I asked myself.

The alarm startled me awake at six o'clock to get ready for the funeral. I cried silently—not for Mike this time, but for what Gil and I do not have together. We are a couple, but we are not close. We support each other as friends, yet we share no passion. I surprised myself with a promise that I would not die before having lived.

Gil rolled over and reminded me that I had to decide what to wear to the funeral. Who cares? was my first thought. I looked at the wrinkled clothes I had slept in, then recalled the dove and the crow. I told Gil about them. He insisted that they were products of my imagination. "They were real," I said loudly, half hoping the volume of my voice would convince him. He didn't respond.

As I put on my bright orange, red, and green autumn-leaf dress, I felt filled with the white light from the night before. Something had changed, and I was different. Three months ago I felt like a stranger in my new body without ovaries and uterus—an unfamiliarity that soon passed. Would this, too, pass, or would it remain with me the rest of my life?

We left Kelli-Lynne at a neighbor's house, explaining that we were going to say good-bye to Mike. I wondered if we were doing the right thing by not taking her, but she was eager to play with her friends and happily kissed me good-bye.

Gil and I arrived thirty minutes early for the funeral, which was to begin at eight o'clock. Men in black suits opened the doors, motioning us into the room. I looked down at Mike in the casket which, like the bags from the hospital, might as well have been marked "Patient's Belongings." If I tried hard, I could connect with his spirit, but I felt no connection to his body.

Little by little, family and friends entered the large room and approached the casket as if Mike were there. With the arrival of the two spokesmen for the church, the final ritual began. Flanked by Gil and my mother, I felt touched and calmed by the blending of religions. The messages were simple: release, heal, continue to love and grow, and revere life, which leads to death. I leaned over and whispered to my mother, "Think of this as Easter come early." She nodded, but her eyes were blank. Was I the only one who had understood?

The Lord's Prayer told me the service was over. People filed past us, viewing Mike's body one last time. They paused to speak to us. Reserved, I felt like a spectator until Mike's classmates marched down the aisle. Then I ached. I strained to see each muscle in their bodies, each rise and fall of their breathing. Searching their eyes, I saw both the terror and the tenderness they felt attending the funeral of someone who only two days before had sat in class with them, joined in the rowdiness in the cafeteria, and complained about the strenuous workouts demanded by the track coach.

I approached the casket last, mindful that I would never see my son again. I had nothing to say, no more to give. My mother joined me and kissed Mike. I did not need to do that now, because I knew Mike was not in his body. At 8:47, I left without turning back.

Because Mike was to be cremated, there would be no burial. Instead, family and friends would be gathering at our house. Gil took my arm, directing me toward the car. "Time to leave," he said. "Let's go home."

I didn't know what to do now that the funeral was over. Would I suddenly snap into being Rosie again, the person I had been before Mike's death? A group of Mike's friends stood on the corner, motionlessly waiting for us to drive by before they returned to school. Wiping the tears from my eyes, I had an urge to rush out and hug each of them and tell them to be careful because life is precious. Instead, I looked at them, and in their eyes I saw they understood life, as well as the suddenness of death. All of us had been touched by death. We were older—innocent no more.

At home, people talked about Mike, filling an invisible album of memories. Everyone had a favorite story to tell. If only we could revive him by pooling our memories, I thought.

"Mike would have pigged out on this food," I murmured to my best friend.

"There wouldn't have been enough if he were here," joked my father, and once more I remembered why my house was crowded with people. I excused myself, rushed to the bathroom, locked the door, turned on the faucet to muffle all sounds, and threw up.

The mail carrier made a special trip three hours earlier than usual. He thought we would be comforted by the many notes addressed to us. His hands shook as he reached out to deposit the pile of cards into my arms. Gil started opening the envelopes, whereupon checks for the scholarship fund dropped out. I didn't want to look at them. Gil read the cards and passed them around. He was managing to keep busy.

Slowly, people left. The telephone was silent. At precisely two o'clock—the time school would be over—I heard footsteps at the back door and automatically jumped up to greet Mike. Four of his friends, including Artie B., stood outside the door. Letting them in, I listened as Artie B. told his story for the first time. After hearing his account, the boys shared tales of Mike. I was fascinated. Their memories were more familiar to me than those of the adults, their pictures fresher. I imagined that we were a group of detectives putting together a puzzle to which each of us held an important piece. We even laughed. What a relief it was to think about Mike in his wholeness—his craziness, his intensity, his humor, and his anger. Meanwhile, Kelli-Lynne darted in and out, glad to be with her big brother's friends. I remarked that Mike would have enjoyed being included in our gathering. Then one boy offered to help with whatever we needed done. I couldn't respond; I didn't know what was needed. I settled into a mist of wanting only Mike.

When the boys left, Kelli-Lynne snuggled up on my lap, saying she had missed our cuddle time. I felt guilty about forgetting our special time together, and I was upset with her because in demanding my attention, she pulled me away from my memories of Mike. How can I attend to both my children at once? I swallowed hard, not sure if I was trying to stop being angry with Kelli-Lynne or to keep from crying. I have enough time for tears when Kelli-Lynne is sleeping, I counseled myself. I squeezed her too tightly, and she squirmed. For a moment, only she and I existed. I wanted a guarantee that nothing would happen to her.

The telephone interrupted this obsession with protecting my only child. It was my brother inviting us to supper, and as I had dreaded preparing the first meal for our family of three, we agreed to go. While I helped Kelli-Lynne change her shirt, she asked what Mikey used to say when he was little and needed help with *his* shirt. It was the first of a flurry of questions about her brother. I couldn't remember what Mike had said. Kelli-Lynne asked on, drafting her own map of understanding.

"Where was I when you, Dad, and Mike lived in Montreal?"

I reminded her that she had not yet been born.

With a giggle, she said, "And now there is you, me, and Dad—so you've always had *one* of us."

How simple she made it all seem. She squirmed, released herself from my grip, looked me straight in the eye, and said, "At least we know where Mike is now." With no hesitation, she challenged, "You told me we would never see Mike again."

"Yes," I said quietly. "I told you that because Mike was dead he would not live with us anymore, and we would never see him again."

"I know, Mom, but you forget that when I die and go to live with God, Mike will be there because I know where he lives now."

I was speechless. Was this the voice of a two and a half year old? She had formed her own connections and her own meaning. I trembled when I realized that for the five minutes I'd been absorbed in conversation with my daughter, Mike's death had been in the background. Still, I felt no relief. I needed to know that by loving my daughter even more deeply, she would not die, too. I couldn't live through another death.

The next morning was the first one with no agenda or company to distract us. We were, for a while at least, a family of three. Kelli-Lynne flopped onto our bed before sunrise. She cupped her hands around my face, saying, "Mom, I'm angry at God because he took Mike away." Before I could respond, she went on. "I would have given Mikey Sudafed or penicillin if he were here. Does God have medicine?"

Waking myself to answer her as honestly as possible, I replied, "No medicine would have helped Mike. He was hurt too badly, and it was too late to give him medicine." I pushed on, searching her face to determine her depth of understanding. "I don't know if God has medicine, but I imagine Mike doesn't need it. God heals without medicine."

She asked earnestly, "Do you think Mikey is teasing God right now the way he always teases me?"

"What do you think?" I asked, buying time to recover from the previous question.

She plunged ahead. "Do you think God is a boy or a girl, or a man or a woman?"

Wearily, I replied, "When I think of God, I imagine a man."

"Good. Mikey would like that." Then she hugged me and curled up beside me, saying, "If Mikey doesn't hurt anymore, I'm glad he is with God." Without another word, she fell asleep.

At about four o'clock, the doorbell rang. It was Peggy, a woman I had met at a workshop six months ago. She knew nothing about Mike's death, and for the first time, I told the whole story. I wasn't aware that her daughter had been killed in a hit-and-run accident fourteen years before. We held each other and cried together, two mothers mourning their children.

Peggy was the first person I ever spoke to who had lived through the death of a child. Listening to her story, I felt as if I were being tutored by a wise woman who carried the authority of experience. Her presence sustained me. On a whim she had driven from Massachusetts to Maine because she hadn't heard from me for a while, and her timing could not have been more perfect. I desperately needed to hear from another mother that it was possible to survive.

Peggy and I spoke softly about the futility of asking why, the necessity of grieving, and my experience of Mike's energy. I told her about the dove and the crow, and she told me I needed to pamper myself. She cautioned me to take small steps, and to avoid making sudden or irrevocable decisions. She also advised Gil and me to find someone objective to guide us in putting our lives back together.

Then I told her how smug I had felt upon recovering from my hysterectomy, believing that somehow I had ensured my right to see my children and their children grow up. "Peggy," I asked, "do you believe that death stalks us, teases us, gives us chances?"

The mail carrier interrupted our conversation with another stack of cards. I urged Peggy to stay, but she insisted that Gil and I needed time together. Stepping outside, she almost bumped into Artie B.'s father, Art, as he made his way to the door. Art handed us a four-page report Artie B. had written for the power company. He said that if we planned to sue the company, he wouldn't release the report. Gil remained silent, so I asserted: "We will not sue. It's senseless to put a price on Mike's life. The money would be worthless. Besides, I can't bear to prolong this ordeal. The wounds would not be able to heal; there would be testimonies, memories that would not sleep, and I refuse to draw that kind of energy to me. Mike is dead. Why torture ourselves and Artie B. and the community?" I sighed. "Most of all, I want to heal, I want to recover, I want to go on. I can't do that by distracting myself with lawsuits."

Suddenly the fog, which had enveloped me for three days, lifted. Art backed toward the door, tears in his eyes. He shook his head, saying, "You people are something else. You were concerned about our son when you learned you own son was dead. I couldn't believe it. And now you're deciding against a financial settlement so you can heal."

I started to tell him there was nothing else we *could* do, but he stumbled out the door, taking the steps two at a time. I could only imagine what his family was going through. Both Artie B. and his brother Scott were Mike's good friends, and now Scott was blaming Artie B. for Mike's death. I could do nothing but try to let go of the past. Suing the power company was not the answer.

Turning away from the door, I sat down to read some of the cards that had come. The words inscribed in them felt like hugs of reassurance:

"To live on in the hearts and memories of those we loved and those who loved us is but one way in which we truly have eternal life."

"I saw your son's death notice in the newspaper, and I felt I must send you a card. I don't know you, but I feel sorry for you."

"We remember Mike well from Nature Camp. My son affectionately called him 'Peach Fuzz.' I remember the day he caught an eel from the stream. Such an enthusiastic and loving boy. . . ."

"Mike was a special kind of person. I can't help but think that he did what he needed to do here, and now it's time to be elsewhere. I'm sure you will be seeing him again."

"I have wanted to telephone you to tell you what a fine son you raised. We really liked Mike, and the loving care with which he was raised was evident in all he did."

"I remember always being impressed with your basic optimism about people and about life. Oh, I do hope that special quality of yours holds you in good stead during this most difficult of times."

Again I was relieved of dinner duty, because on the spur of the moment we went off to visit my parents. Kelli-Lynne played while we talked. When the conversation turned to the downed power line, my father exploded. He was furious that we had not heard from the power company. And he was angry with us for deciding not to initiate legal action. "A lawsuit is exactly what they deserve," he spat.

"I don't. Mike doesn't," I explained softly. "I want no more children electrocuted. An educational campaign would be more healing than a vengeful lawsuit," I added with passion.

Then I told my parents we were planning to scatter Mike's ashes at a local beach on the fourth of May—the day he had set aside for his first boy-girl party, in celebration of his fifteenth birthday. The beach we chose, I explained, was at Two Lights State Park, which had been special to all four of us.

Mom objected to scattering Mike's ashes at Two Lights. "There will be no visiting place," she moaned. Then she asked if we would consider scattering the ashes in three separate places.

I wanted all of Mike's ashes sprinkled in one place—the ocean he loved. With a strength I didn't know I possessed, I said I would not separate the ashes that were once Mike's body. Somewhere deep inside me rose the advice, Move through this with integrity. The decision was mine to make; he was my son.

The conversation drifted into memories. We reflected on how differently Mike had acted the last three weeks of his life. Everyone had enjoyed being with him. It seemed to all of us that he had let go of the sullenness and the you-can't-tell-me-anything attitude that had marked most of his fourteenth year. How surprised I was when he had kissed his sister good night for the first time in many months and when I learned of his detailed plans for my surprise birthday party. His pouting had been replaced with conversation. Everyone had noticed the change, but we didn't dare comment on it for fear of provoking a regression.

The last half hour of Mike's life had been fun filled and loving. He, Kelli-Lynne, Artie B., and I had munched on homemade crackers and giggled. The boys had tried to decide how to divide the money they had earned that morning shoveling snow. Their ideas ranged from banking the whole amount to throwing a party, buying a new fly rod, or sending me to cooking school so the bread I was trying to make wouldn't be recycled into crackers. What a relief it was to be joking rather than arguing. Looking back, it seems as if death had waited until Mike had taken on a more positive outlook.

We talked with my parents for so long that we decided to stay overnight with them. Memories, I discovered, don't sleep. In the guest room—my old bedroom—I was greeted by a picture of Mike at twenty months of age. I wept.

The next day at the beach, I learned that tears do not freeze. Kelli-Lynne was full of life and innocence. Mom commented on the coming of spring; and indeed, buds on the trees signaled that another season was unfolding. Yet, all I could focus on was my dead son. Kelli-Lynne reminded me of my own youth and innocence, and the hours of freedom I had spent playing on the beach, but winter remained in my heart.

Later we joined friends for our traditional Sunday deck breakfast. Our daughters jumped up and down when they saw each other. Frazzled because Kelli-Lynne had wet her pants on the short ride over, I fell apart. Joan changed Kelli-Lynne after handing me a cup of coffee. Marge reached out for my hand. I felt separated from my closest friends, as if I had been branded with a luminous symbol announcing to everyone that I was the mother of a dead son. I looked around to see if anyone was staring at me with my branded heart, but no one was. Anxious, fumbling motions were familiar to me now, as were streams of unspoken questions. When will the strain disappear? How do I begin to talk? How much do they want to hear? Is it painful for them to listen, to think that it might have been one of *their* children who had died?

Death is an intruder in the neighborhood. Mike's death invaded each of our lives. I wondered what I could talk about without breaking down.

Someone told the children to go upstairs. Sarah, Joan's two-and-a-half-year-old daughter, motioned for me to pick her up. She whispered in my ear, "Mike is dead, you know."

I hugged her close and said, "Yes, I know."

"Now there will be lots more bacon for all of us because Mike used to eat most of it."

Marge hugged me and started to cry. We all sighed, and then our friends spoke about the Mike they knew.

Don and Dave reminisced about their many fishing trips, and about how excited Mike had been to catch and cook a six-pound bluefish. They recalled Mike's tendency to attach inflated prices to the paraphernalia he wanted to get rid of at neighborhood yard sales, then become insulted when customers offered anything less. We women talked about how disgusting and unnatural he thought it was for us to nurse our babies. Joan recalled with laughter how obstinate and unappreciative he had been during a special night out we had for him at one of his favorite restaurants. In no way would he enjoy himself.

Gil and Don reminisced about the day Mike and Artie B. had pedaled their bicycles twenty miles to my parents' home to prove they could do it. We laughed about how worried I had been. Four hours after their departure they had called to announce their arrival. When Gil and I drove out to pick them up, I was furious, mentally tracing the busy highway they had traveled along. The moment we saw Mike, he began boasting of his accomplishment, the adrenaline in his system still rushing, and talking about how confused he was by my anger. He had realized a dream and expected congratulations; and I was responding to a nightmare that never happened.

It was impossible to put Mike on a pedestal. He had a strong personality that insisted on expression. Each one of us had been witness to his lack of patience with the young children, his reluctance to take advice, his daring ways of asserting his individuality, and his efforts to break away so he could be by himself. And we laughed about how incessantly he had teased our girls.

Marge reminded me that I hated to be the disciplinarian. I did, but I knew Mike lacked common sense and needed someone to set limits for him. I recalled the many times I had punished him, and how often I regretted my strictness. Yet, I had no choice. And ultimately I was right: his lack of common sense had *killed* him. Only this time, I didn't have the satisfaction of saying, "I told you so. That's exactly what I was worried about."

When the children demanded food, we went to our posts, as we had done so many times before. One person squeezed fresh orange juice, another buttered the bagels. I measured out coffee and started the bacon sizzling. Marge separated the eggs. Dave and Don set the table on the sundeck. Our breakfast preparations had become so automatic that Dave ended up setting one extra place at the table. No one noticed until we sat down. The plate glared at us. Wordlessly, we agreed to leave it there. Nobody remembered to adjust the proportions either, and we had mounds of leftovers.

"Mike had a huge appetite," I acknowledged as the meal drew to a close. Saying what I was thinking felt sane, whereas continuing to keep all comments to myself would have driven me crazy.

Conversation turned to the community garden. Mike had ordered and planted seeds, labeled them, and lined them up in his room. Not only that, but he had sketched a map illustrating where they should be planted. He was well ahead of the rest of us. While the others at the table talked about plans for the garden, I realized how much I wanted to transplant Mike's seedlings. Unable to face the task alone, however, I asked Joan and Marge to help me. How would I feel eating the vegetables he had started? I couldn't save my son, I decided, but I could ensure the life of the seeds he had planted. They, at least, would blossom.

"S-spring is officially here," I stammered, "and it used to be my favorite season. Now Mike's death is all mixed up with spring. The seeds he planted and his death are all mixed up for me."

Kelli-Lynne came over and patted me on the back. She asked if I was missing Mike. "Yes," I replied.

"Oh," she said, "but you're not choking."

We went home around noon. Once Kelli-Lynne was settled in bed for a nap, Gil and I were alone. I sighed. In answer, Gil said he was going out to stack wood. I stood up and caught my reflection in the mirror over the mantle. I stared at my face. My eyes were wide open and sunken. Circles of darkness were carved on my otherwise expressionless face. My hair was uncombed and greasy, my clothes wrinkled. For the first time in five days, I saw myself. Why hadn't anyone told me how ghastly I looked? I glanced from the mirror to the pictures of Mike. Our eyes looked the same, only his sparkled and mine had dimmed.

I retreated to the bathroom, turned on the bathwater, poured in a generous amount of bubble bath, lit my favorite candle, and sank into the perfumed water. The fragrance from the soap beads reminded me of the scented air at the wake. I sank deeper into the water. Slowly, I washed my body. My movements were no longer automatic: I watched myself struggle to remember how to take a bath.

After getting dressed, I called my friend Anne in Ohio. Time to share my tragedy. As soon as she answered the phone, I blurted out, "Mike is dead." I said the words again and braced myself for her reaction, but I heard only silence. I knew that Anne was recalling the death of her first husband, which was followed closely by the death of her ten-day-old daughter.

Finally Anne said, "I was in Buffalo, New York, on Friday, and almost drove to Maine to see you. I called several times, but your line was always busy." She went on to describe her experiences with death. Listening to her, I felt included in a sorority—a response similar to the one I had felt as older women shared stories of their hysterectomies. But, I wondered, must this always be a sorority of suffering?

"Damn, this is not what I had planned," I said. "What did I do wrong?" Then I lied and told Anne I had accepted Mike's death. I meant only that I had survived the funeral, that I had buried him. No, I reminded myself, that isn't true either. The scattering of his ashes is a month away. Damn, I don't know what I mean.

Anne's voice jolted me back to our conversation. "Rosie, you should never feel that you have accepted his death."

When I didn't respond, she volunteered to come stay with me, but I didn't want to have to please one more person. More importantly, I was afraid of becoming an emotional invalid; I wanted to return to normal.

I said, as though reading a script, "I know the healing has to come from within, and I don't want to lean on anyone right now." I hung up, knowing Anne would alert other friends who would soon be calling.

Quickly I phoned Bill, whom I had met while teaching at the Creative Problem Solving Institute (CPSI) in Buffalo. How would I tell him? How would he react? No need to wonder—I reached his answering service. I left my name, number, and a brief message: "Urgent." I had met Bill's two daughters, but he hadn't met Mike. And now he never would. What do I want from Bill? Simply for him to know, I decided. That's enough.

When the telephone rang, I was happy to hear Bill's voice. After I told him what had happened, he exploded, "Goddamn son of a bitch!" I was unprepared for the ensuing volley of four-letter words. His shouting scared me and reminded me that I had not voiced my own rage. I listened, squirming inside, knowing that if I were to grieve Bill's way, I would groan and sob and scream from deep inside, and punch until I dropped. I wanted to interrupt him with, "But what about *me?*"

He must have read my mind. His voice softened as he said, "Rosie, I want to reach out and touch you, and walk on the beach with you and drink beer."

"Me, too," I whispered, comforted by this image. He promised to send me energy.

I made one more call—to Bob, coauthor of a book we were writing for teachers. Our planned work schedule for the book, I knew, would have to be changed. How could I concentrate on writing when I couldn't remember how to take a bath? Bob neither exploded nor offered advice. He said he was shocked and concerned, and would send the final drafts of four chapters as planned. His way of grieving was to keep working. I told him I would try to complete my part of the writing, but I made no promises.

Everyone I had spoken with thus far had a prescription for grief. I alternated between swallowing them all simultaneously and refusing to try any of them. I had no idea what my own remedy was. In the meantime, I kept moving. Movement, at least, ran counter to death.

I was grateful to go drink tea in the late afternoon with an eighty-one-year-old woman who lives up the street. Mike used to shovel her driveway. She told me about the deaths of her husband and daughter, and how she had coped and changed. She said the emptiness in her heart had never disappeared entirely. Her wisdom sobered me. Until then I had held tightly to a fantasy of being completely healed sometime in the future. According to my octogenarian mentor, the pain of not seeing Mike on a daily basis would dull, but I would never be able to erase his existence. I listened intently and was soothed, trusting that I did not have to fill the empty space in my heart. A hole will be forever a part of my wholeness.

The tea warmed my body. I slowed down. Hearing that I would never finish grieving gave me occasion to pause. I hugged her when I left, and she invited me to come back whenever I felt like "a warm fire and hot tea with an old lady."

While walking home, I met up with some neighbors who were on their way to my house. They looked at me, studying my face for clues that would help them know what to say. They handed me a card and a check for the scholarship fund. As we talked, another friend pulled her car into my driveway. She had brought a plant for me. I didn't know what to do. I no longer remembered how to make small talk. How do I explain that I want company sometimes, but I don't want to entertain or even speak? Would they all think I was crazy if I invited them in to listen to music?

As I was trying to decide what to say, I noticed Tim, one of Mike's friends, circling the house on his bike. I waved to him, and he approached. The women said good-bye and left me standing alone on the steps. I smiled at Tim, and he apologized for fainting at Mike's funeral. "I didn't mean to do it," he said. "It just happened. I've never fainted in my life. I hope I didn't ruin everything."

I assured him quietly that he hadn't ruined anything for me. I wasn't even aware of the incident, which made me wonder what else I had missed. We talked about Mike for a few minutes, then he asked, somewhat embarrassedly, if he could play with Kelli-Lynne. "Mike would have wanted us to play with her, to look out for her," he said simply.

I nodded my head, pleased by his thoughtfulness. Before he disappeared into the house, he said over his shoulder, "I hope you don't think I'm queer or anything because I want to play with her. I don't know how to 'un-miss' Mike, and being with Kelli-Lynne is like being close to Mike."

"Come as often as you like," I replied. "She will be thrilled." While listening to them playing in the den, I felt a gnawing pain shoot through me. Why isn't it Mike in there teasing her? I wanted to scream. How easily I could imagine that the sounds I heard were Kelli-Lynne and her brother!

Lulled by the familiar noise in the den, I stared out the kitchen window. The two plant pots Mike had given me for my thirty-third birthday framed the window facing the school yard. The pots, I had decided at the time, symbolized Mike's growing ability to express his love. My focus shifted from the window to the school yard, in which kids were now playing on the spot where he died. I vowed that Kelli-Lynne would not attend school next door.

I appreciated the cards, calls, and visits from Mike's classmates. Their courage and sensitivity had bolstered me, and I wanted to publicly acknowledge the importance of their support. But why am I able to permit others to grieve, I wondered, while not granting myself the same favor?

April 1, 1977

$\mathcal{A}$ new week, the calendar announced—a week uninterrupted by death. I promised to make this week as normal as possible by returning to my exercise class. Driving was scary, because I had to concentrate on every movement in advance. I recalled how I had roused myself to take a shower an hour after Kelli-Lynne was born. I recited each individual step: turn on the water, unwrap the soap, take a washcloth, soap the body. The trauma of death, like that of birth, has left me with no automatic reactions.

Aware of my limits, I drove very carefully. I switched on the radio and froze in response to the news flash of a fifteen-year-old boy who had been killed by a hit-and-run driver. I swerved to the side of the road, my knuckles white and my fingers glued to the steering wheel. I looked in the mirror at my deathly pale face. Did he suffer? I wondered.

My mother was planning to meet me at exercise class. I had made a commitment to be there. Still, I was reluctant to drive on, loath to return to familiar routines. Another mother is now sentenced to what I am going through, I thought.

In class I was anonymous. Nobody knew about Mike. The familiar faces lulled me into believing that life goes on. Mom and I kept our eyes on each other. After a while, however, I overheard her confiding to a few women that her grandson had died. I looked away when she pointed at me. I respected Mom's right to deal with her agony in her own way, but I preferred anonymity. Instead of asking her to stop telling people about my son, I kicked my legs till they ached. The twisting and flexing felt good. I obliterated all thoughts by concentrating on exercises that were once as familiar to me as hanging out clothes. "Discipline is important," I said aloud, suddenly realizing how much I had changed in one week.

After class I busied myself around the house. Kelli-Lynne and a friend played in the sandbox with a Noah's Ark game I had ordered for her the same day I had ordered Life for Mike. I, meanwhile, went through the motions of vacuuming, and washing dishes and clothes. The routine took all my concentration. To avoid feeling my pain, I told myself I would forever set the table for three. "Forever" reminded me of all the words I was exorcising from my vocabulary—words like *guarantee, happiness, normal,* and *hope.* I used to be idealistic. I used to have a son. I used to live in a present that had a future. Now I have no sense of promise.

With everything spic-and-span at home, it was time to visit the junior high school Mike had attended for three years. I wanted his classmates to know that their courage in coming to the funeral enabled me to get through it. I had tried to write each of them a letter, but my heart rebelled against the impersonal. Hence, today's mission: to announce our thanks over the PA system.

As Gil and I pushed through the creaking front door, I recounted the many times I'd entered this building. Mike would forget his lunch money, or a book for class, or his bathing suit on the day of a swim meet. I could almost mesmerize myself into believing this was another emergency visit to school, but my shoulders were heavy, my head throbbed like a beating drum, and my throat was dry.

It was almost dismissal time. Teenagers stood in small groups lining the corridors. Quietly I asked Gil if he had prepared anything to say. He didn't answer. It seemed strange that having decided to express our thanks to Mike's classmates, we hadn't discussed what our message would be.

The principal greeted us and tried to make us comfortable. He confided that our request to address the students had come as a surprise. Then he read through several announcements while I waited numb and terrified, steadily convincing myself that I would be unable to resurrect what I wanted to say. The principal motioned to us. Gil spoke first, and his voice sounded steady and strong. I was proud of him. When he finished, he motioned to me. I tried to speak from my heart. I don't recall my words, but when I looked around, the principal, the secretaries, and a few students were crying.

Our next stop was Mike's English classroom to pick up an autobiography he had written. In the corridor, I was struck by the absence of noise: no rowdiness, no excited voices, no kids racing to the bus. Artie B.'s brother, Scott, had waited by the office door to lead us to Mike's classroom, then he waited outside to go home with us, silently saying, "I'm here. I'm not Mike, but I'm here."

I longed to read Mike's autobiography immediately, but Gil and I had one more stop before heading home: we wanted to thank Gil's boss for his support. Walking into his office, I was assaulted by pictures of his two kids displayed on the walls. My cheeks were wet. He pointed to a bio-rhythm chart he had run on Mike. He explained that according to the chart, March 23—the day of Mike's death—signified "a double crossover for physical and intellectual processes," a time to exercise extreme cau-tion. I didn't pretend to understand. Mike is dead, I told myself. The bio-rhythm chart is too late. Still, I shelved the knowledge in the area of my consciousness labeled Evidential Signs of Mike Hall's Death, appreciating the opportunity to add another fact to the enigma that was Mike.

When we finally got home I collapsed into bed and let Gil take care of Kelli-Lynne. Although I had closed the bedroom door, the sounds of the telephone and people's voices penetrated my restless sleep. I could not will myself to get up. Besides, I did not have the strength to relate to people. I had said everything I had to say.

Still lying down, I forced myself to read Mike's autobiography. The sight of his handwriting sent chills down my body. I imagined his voice reading to me: "I started swimming competitively last year, and I have loved it ever since. Yet, as I think about how much I looked forward to swimming sessions, I remember how I felt after the first night of practice. There was only a fine line between giving up or going on. I thought about it and decided to go on. This is a decision I follow many times now. It is always easier to quit something, but in the long run, you usu-ally lose. Thus, when I think of dropping biology, I say to myself, 'No, you can hack it.' I think this is one of the most important things in life, not quitting when you are down."

Then why did you die? were the words I wanted to scream at him.

Gil came in to say good night, then announced he would be sleep-ing upstairs "so we won't disturb each other." I understood this to mean that our public appearances as the loving couple had ended.

About midnight, I noticed my body pulsating with energy. My heart-beat accelerated, and I felt scared and alert. Bright lights filled the room. I closed my eyes tightly, then opened them a little to see if the lights had disappeared. They hadn't. Cautiously peeking through half-open eyes, I became mesmerized by a bright orange spiral light circling about a pure white center that had a minute black dot in the middle of it. As I watched closely, the brilliant orange border gradually turned yellow, the vivid center remaining unchanged.

Jolted, I sat up in bed. I didn't understand how or why, but I recog-nized the energy contained in the colors. My heart responded to this energy, and I knew it was similar to that of my own heart's light. Understanding exploded as I realized that this light was somehow related to Mike. Without warning I began to float, and for an instant I wondered if I was dying, but I relaxed, knowing for the first time ever that I did not fear death.

While floating, I experienced myself as a concentrated point of energy. I traveled easily through space, aware of Mike as pure essence and of myself as an aspect of that essence.

As if in affirmation, Mike's vibrations responded to my own with: "That's right, Mom. There is no difference. No division, no separation."

We were communicating! Somehow I was able to interpret his message even though it was not spoken; similarly, he was able to hear the questions in my mind although I hadn't uttered them out loud.

"Proof is irrelevant, Mom. What is compelling is your understanding of the impression you are receiving. Together we have activated a link. I have some information for you and others that will sustain you and bring new light to you."

In that moment I knew with absolute clarity that one of us had had to die in order to connect in this way. I thought, "I really did love you, Mike, even though I didn't know how to show it."

"I know," he replied. "We shared that too. No need to forgive or forget. Regain your faith in cosmic laws. Realize with all your being that there are no mistakes. There is no need for blame or accusation. There is only clear understanding."

I reflected on the qualities we had shared: we looked alike, we carried ourselves in the same manner, and we defended ourselves in similar ways. Our limitations were defined by our humanness, nothing more.

I knew intuitively that the "information" he was speaking of referred to messages of reassurance that I was to relay to the family. Like a good mother, I advised Mike to deliver his own truths, but I also understood that for some reason he was not in contact with other members of the family. Why me? I wanted to ask. Why can I channel your energy while others cannot?

"Very simple," he replied in a dance of energy. "You recognize and welcome spirit. You have been a student of spirit for a long time—longer than you know. I am now inspirited, and you do not fear me or dismiss me."

I agreed to deliver the messages he was about to send, but I was afraid I would forget them by morning.

"Don't worry, Mom," Mike signaled, as if prompted by my thoughts. "I'll give you a memory sign."

His easy humor and uncharacteristic patience intrigued me. Our roles had changed! I was to be his messenger; he, my teacher. I felt a rush of energy as this awareness surged through me.

Mike showed me his gifts to the family. For his grandfather, he displayed an image of a white glove topped by two crossed, sparkling silver swords with brass hilts. "He will understand the glove's connection with his Masonic ritual," Mike instructed. In addition, he showed me the mast of a ship flanked by three flags and an upright compass. "It doesn't make sense to you," Mike admonished before I had a chance say I was confused. To his grandmother he gave a bouquet of marigolds and a huge, baked Thanksgiving turkey. To Gil and me he gave the simple message, "I am linked."

Mike complimented me on my powers of locomotion—"transport," he called it—and on my ability to receive information telepathically. I wasn't used to compliments from him. In life, we seldom admitted that we were influenced by each other. My heart understood that Mike was practicing to be a healer, and that I was to benefit from his education.

At two-thirty in the morning, I awoke to shapes of the gifts silhouetted against the bedroom windows. Clearly I had not been dreaming, I told myself. I was secure in the knowledge that Mike was finding his own way yet wanting to help those of us who were here. Recalling the integrity and ease of our exchange, I rolled over and slept peacefully for the first time in five nights.

I don't know how to make sense of these nighttime occurrences that bring me close to Mike. Even so, I carry the memory of his nocturnal visits into my waking life. I inhabit two worlds and don't know which one is real. How can I mourn my son when I feel such a close connection to him? Do *all* parents go through this?

In the morning I got out of bed and called my parents to deliver the messages. My father answered, and didn't respond when I told him what had happened. Mom, on the other hand, seemed intrigued, and asked why Mike appeared to me and not to her.

"I don't know," I said quietly. "I'm only doing what I promised to do." On a nonrational level, I knew that Mike and I had made a commitment to each other a long time ago. I shivered at the thought.

Next I called my grandfather. He was the one person in the family who would talk to me about other ways of knowing. He had let me down, however, by not attending the wake, or even calling me. I felt abandoned by him, though I knew he had adored Mike.

Nanny answered, and got nervous when I asked to speak to Bomp. She cautioned me not to upset him. Bomp's voice stirred up words from deep within me. "I understand you spent the early morning hours with Mike," I said, unaware of how I knew this.

"Yep," he replied, not the least bit surprised by my greeting. "He's okay, Rosalie. He is progressing, and he needs us to be accepting. He needs us to help him leave and continue on."

"He is becoming a healer, Bomp." Once again I was surprised by my words. What a relief it was to talk with someone who understood. My grandfather asked for no explanations: our shared experience bonded us. Only after hanging up did I realize I had failed to tell him how angry I was that he had not come to the funeral. But then, that was part of the past. I had survived; Bomp had survived; and Mike's energy had survived.

Next I called my friend Carole, who was accustomed to working in the world of spirit. I wanted to hear the news she had of Mike. Carole explained that as soon as she had heard about Mike's death, she tuned into his energy. Struck by his disorientation, she sent furthering energy, as I had at the hospital. A few hours later, she tuned in again. By then he was unencumbered and evolving.

"He is our teacher now," I said with emotion in my voice.

Carole went on to explain that she had asked for more information from spirit the following day. She was told that Mike had always had one foot in the spiritual realm, as is true of many highly intelligent people. At a crucial point the intellectual and the physical processes synthesize, her sources explained, and after this transition is complete, there is no longer a need to live in the physical dimension. The realm of spirit becomes the world of graduation, they told her.

"And that's why he is a teacher and a healer," I said easily. I shivered at the connection.

April 4, 1977

*M*arge and Joan came over to help me transplant Mike's seedlings into larger containers for the community garden.

"I don't know why these plants mean so much to me," I told them, "but they do. I want to carry out Mike's plans. At least I can have a hand in something that is growing."

"Rosie, it doesn't matter why," Marge replied, hugging me. "We know it's important for you to do this, and we're glad you invited us to help."

I smiled, relieved to know I did not have to figure out the answers. While our three daughters played in the living room, we transferred the hundreds of seedlings into large containers, watered them carefully, and talked about Mike. Although most of the original cups had been labeled, several boxes of seedlings had not. I like the idea of being surprised by what Mike has planted.

April 7, 1977

Today I drove to the pharmacy to pick up the photographs we took at my birthday party last month. These pictures, I knew, would remind me of Mike's final celebration. I waited impatiently in line. At last I gave the woman behind the counter the order number, whereupon she stepped into a back room and returned with a package and a puzzled look on her face. "No charge," she said.

"What do you mean, 'No charge'?" I asked.

"Apparently, the roll of film didn't develop," she replied.

I grabbed the packet, drove to a small print-developing company, and asked the manager if *he* would develop the pictures. Looking over the roll I handed him, he said, "Lady, you must have used outdated film. You don't have pictures here."

The pictures didn't develop. The bread I was making the day Mike died didn't rise. The seedlings we carefully transplanted died within two days. Whatever I try to hold on to disappears.

April 10, 1977

My heart is broken. I am shadowed by death. I waver between wanting everyone I see to know about Mike's death and wishing everyone who knows would forget. There is a huge gulf now between me and my friends. I feel guilty, angry, scared, confused, and numb. Within seconds, one feeling explodes into another like a firecracker. All the while I talk in a monotone.

The thought that Kelli-Lynne might die preoccupies me. Maybe if I had been more alert, more conscientious, more patient—I torture myself searching for the unspoken, the undone, the lost opportunity to have made a difference between Mike alive and Mike dead. How do I begin again without my oldest child? How can I be present for Kelli-Lynne when I am numbed by grief?

And what about my relationship with Gil? Our marriage was floundering *before* Mike's death. How can we begin to talk now without being ripped farther apart? My heart aches. I am tired of pretending I am strong, yet I am afraid to break down.

I fought hard to ensure Mike's birth. At seventeen I was in love. I'd been in love for three years, and wanted to get out of my house. Andy was two years older. Pregnant as a senior, I left high school in disgrace; my friends acted as if I didn't exist. Andy and I got married, and I pretended to be happy. Living in a one-room apartment while my husband attended college, I pretended I could cope. Pregnancy shattered my illusions.

Mike was born in the hospital the moment the bell rang to announce the end of the school day. Friends visited me there, but they were strangers; four months had gone by since I had heard from them. They wanted to know what it was like to be married and to give birth. I, on the other hand, wondered: When did I become "legitimate"? How can they pretend we are still friends after such a long interlude of silence? My most immediate thought was, How dare they expect me to share the intimacies of my birth experience! Yet, I joined the masquerade by pretending all was well. That week my friends were preparing for graduation while I was learning to change diapers.

Mike's birth came at a price. I sacrificed my late adolescence. I grew accustomed to compromise. I was divorced before I turned nineteen.

Commuting to college as a single mother of a one year old, I couldn't devote much time to my studies or to socializing, and I couldn't be 100 percent mother, either. Nor could I live on my own; I had too many responsibilities. I lived with my parents, acted like I was satisfied and could withstand the pain, but at night I cried alone.

If offered the chance to relive my life, I would choose to give birth to Mike regardless of all I'd have to give up. But God, it isn't fair that in the end I had to give *him* up.

April 16, 1977

This morning I was determined to clean Mike's room. I didn't want to do it alone, and I didn't want Gil to think I was weak if I asked for his help. I asked anyway.

"Rose, I have to go to work," he replied.

I pleaded, "But I need you here—especially today. I don't want to go into that room alone."

Gil shrugged and said he would be home for lunch as usual.

"Does that mean you'll help after lunch?" I asked.

"Rose, I already told you. I have work to think about."

As I watched him drive away, I stamped my foot on the floor. How dare he leave me alone, I roared. Then I stomped around the kitchen mustering the courage to face the empty, cluttered bedroom that had been Mike's. Kelli-Lynne, with her "blankie" in hand, joined me. I yanked out several large plastic bags, rolling up my sleeves as if preparing for a fight.

His room looked normal: a stack of dirty clothes in one corner, fishing rods and lures in another, stamps scattered everywhere, coin containers tossed haphazardly on his bureau, lists of all sorts strewn across his desk, and an open journal shoved under his bed. I wasn't prepared to see his handwriting, especially in a journal. Questions surfaced: Do I dare read it? Do I have the right to? What if it says that he hated me? Worse yet, what if he had planned his death and left a parting message here for me to see?

Hungrily, I devoured the words as if Mike lived on in the pages. The last entry was dated January 1977: "School rots. New Year's resolution—no fingernail biting. Broke one set in track."

The previous entry was dated January 1, 12:00 AM: "Went fishing at North Pond. Caught one perch, happy to get home."

I hugged myself, delighted that he was happy to be home. After looking around unsuccessfully for more journals, I decided to begin packing up clothes. Goodwill would benefit. With energy I didn't know I possessed, I swept through the drawers and the closet. Five bags later, I had finished with the clothes and began crating the books on his shelves. I saved his rock polisher and metal detector.

All this time Kelli-Lynne was following me around. At last she asked if she could sleep "in Mikey's bed forever." I hesitated, not knowing what was right.

"Can this be *my* room now, Mom?"

I hesitated again. She disappeared, and I continued to clear out Mike's things. The telephone rang, and I went to answer it. When I got back, there was Kelli-Lynne, curled up with her three favorite stuffed animals, asleep in Mike's bed. "Thank God for her," I whispered. She looked so tiny and innocent. How I wished I could join her.

Ten trips later, all the evidence revealing that Mike Hall had ever lived in this top bedroom was erased. I had accomplished something that needed to be done and I wanted to feel satisfied, but I felt guilty. Maybe I should have waited longer before cleaning his room. Waited for what? I wondered.

April 22, 1977

When I picked up my friend Bill at the airport today, I was jolted into remembering all the times Mike and Gil had been there to meet me. This was my first trip to the airport since Mike's death, and it was not easy. Someone had warned me about anxiety arising in "the firsts"—the first Easter, the first birthday, the first Mother's Day, the first day of school, the first Thanksgiving, the first Christmas. Indeed, the first time I went to the post office, I instinctively asked for a block of stamps for Mike's collection. What will I do the first time someone asks how many children I have?

April 23, 1977

It's been a month since Mike died. Does one celebrate the anniversary of a death?

Today was the second day of a chanting workshop I helped to sponsor. Six of us had been planning the workshop for months, and although my life is nothing like it was in the organizing stages of the event, I understood instinctively that I had to be there because Mike's soul needed music.

The chants, led by David Zeller, whom I had met last year at the annual Humanistic Psychology conference in Princeton, New Jersey, seemed tailored to what I believed both Mike and I needed to hear. While strumming his guitar, David began simply: "Listen, listen, listen to my heart's song. / Listen, listen, listen to my heart's song. / I will never forget you, I will never forsake you. . . ." Upon first hearing this chant, I thought the three words at the end of the first and second lines were "my hard song." Being in my heart, I acknowledged, is hard right now. Pain resounds.

David continued: "Spirit is around us like a rainbow 'round the sun." The words conjured an image of Mike, *my* son, surrounded by a rainbow of spirit. Tears moistened my face. Immersed in the chord sequences, I suddenly realized that I didn't know anything about the rhythm of my life without Mike. Music creates a sound mandala, and the center is the sacred void.

I wondered if I should be there. I am supposed to be grieving, I told myself. Do I have a right to be set free? And then I got angry. How dare you set me free, Mike, I wanted to scream. I had an urge to escape, but decided to sit through one more song. A friend squeezed my hand and smiled.

"Thanks. I needed that," I told her, aware of how rapidly my emotions were swinging from peacefulness to anger to guilt.

David sang: "Children are the not-yet-realized people. / To the gods they belong. . . ." I nodded, feeling this truth in my heart. I did know that Mike never belonged to me. I had never thought of him as my possession. I just didn't know where *I* belonged *without* him.

April 24, 1977

Last night in my dream I was an observer, watching and waiting. Cupped hands were encircling a chalice. I didn't understand the meaning of this image, although I imagined it was religious. My heart responds by feeling warm, but my mind makes no connections.

April 25, 1977

I've read some of Elisabeth Kübler-Ross's material on death and dying. Her focus is more on dying than on grieving. The ordeal of parents who have suddenly lost a child is not well documented anywhere. I know I have to learn through experience. The last four months have catapulted me beyond any learning I could have acquired from books or from people. Life and death are my teachers.

My brother was here today. He brusquely announced that his wife is five weeks pregnant. He was excited. I was angry. Could they have conceived a child, I wondered, on the night Mike died? My feelings were irrational, and I was jealous, too. She is pregnant with life; I am heavy with death.

April 27, 1977

*A*nother first. This one was a dentist appointment. The last few appointments were for Mike, but today our family dentist never mentioned him. The lack of acknowledgment was worse than anything he could have said.

I was still upset about the dentist when I went to meet a friend for lunch. Our waitress was one of Mike's childhood babysitters. No matter what I do, I bump into the past. At first I didn't want her to say anything. Then, when she said how much she had been thinking about me and Mike, I saw how quickly my needs shift. Nothing feels right at the time it occurs.

April 29, 1977

*F*lux. Everything has changed so suddenly that I no longer know what to believe. When Kelli-Lynne pulls my head down to touch her face and asks if I will promise to be her mommy forever and ever, I don't know how to answer her. I want to be both truthful and simple. I imagine she needs the assurance that I will not die and leave her. I want to say the right thing to make life easier for her, but I have to be honest. How do I know if I'll be alive tomorrow? So I reach out and hold her, and whisper to both of us, "Yes, I will be your mother forever and ever."

"Even if you're dead, you will still be my mother, Mom?"

"Yes, I promise I will. I will not forget I'm your mother even when I'm dead." Satisfied, she squirms out of my arms to chase the cat.

What do I do with this foreboding that shadows my heart? Every time the telephone rings, I expect to be told someone else I love has died. I used to be optimistic, idealistic, even naive. Now I expect bad news.

Logotherapist Viktor Frankel's statement "To live is to suffer, to survive is to find meaning in the suffering" is one I have never wanted to believe. Until now.

May 4, 1977

Today is, or would have been, Mike's fifteenth birthday—the day for scattering his ashes at Two Lights. Last night I had a dream in which Mike told me to place his ashes in a creel that was buried under a pile of clothes in a large cylinder in the garage. "The creel is important, Mom, because I am a fisherman," Mike said.

The dream was so real to me that when I woke up, I tiptoed barefoot to the garage. Hidden in a corner was a large round packing case just like the one in the dream. Trancelike, I pried off the lid and found stacks of outgrown clothes. I pulled out the clothes until my hands grasped a solid object at the bottom of the barrel. "This must be the creel," I whispered. It was an odd-shaped straw bucket with a slit in the top, and it had a ruler attached to it. For years Mike had used this to measure his fish and carry them home. My grandfather had given it to him for his fifth birthday.

Slowly and carefully, I fingered the rough edges, stunned that I had dreamed a dream that was real. Is Mike in touch with me? Is he directing me, reassuring me, giving me signs? Death has no reality for me as long as I have this connection, I mused. I looked down at the creel in my hands. If the dream and the creel were real, what does that say about my relationship with Mike? I dizzy myself with thinking.

Gil was in the kitchen when I quietly closed the back door behind me. "Mike's creel," I said, showing him my discovery. "For the ashes."

"Where did you find *that?*" Gil asked. "I haven't seen it in years."

I told him where I had found it. He looked at me oddly, and I pushed on, needing to tell someone. "Actually, Gil, I dreamed that Mike told me to put his ashes in the creel because he was a fisherman. So I took his advice and found the creel in the garage. It's important to follow Mike's wishes."

I desperately wanted Gil to say he believed me. Instead, he shrugged his shoulders and left the kitchen.

A knock at the door jolted me out of my quandary. Setting the creel on the mantle, beside the vase that held Mike's ashes, I went to see who had come. It was Michael Dwinell, the priest who had assisted at Mike's funeral. "Rosie," he said, "I don't know why I'm here, but I felt the urge to see how you are doing."

I glanced at the dark, ash-filled urn that had been on the mantle for six days. "Today is Mike's birthday," I announced in confusion. "At least, it always *was*. We are going to scatter his ashes. And I had a dream last night about how to do it. I don't understand why, but Mike's death and my life seem all tangled up."

Michael smiled at me. "Okay, Rosie, now I understand why I've come. Did anyone at the funeral home tell you to be prepared to see bone fragments or maybe teeth particles mixed in with the ashes?"

I held my breath. Never before had I thought about my son's body being destroyed by fire.

"Rosie, I just don't want you to be surprised by the ashes."

"But, Michael, I'm not afraid. You see, I feel connected to Mike in a different way. I do understand he is not in his body. The voice I heard in my dream was *his*."

All day I felt filled with faith, supported in my knowledge of another reality that exists side by side with death. How could I believe in the finality of death and in my dreams at the same time? I was prepared to carry out the empty ritual while holding a different truth in my heart.

My parents, brother, sister-in-law, Gil, Kelli-Lynne, and I walked together to Two Lights. "One last ritual," I whispered. I told everyone about my dream; no one responded. Instinctively I headed toward the large rock Mike had claimed nine years ago as his mountain island. The sides of the rock were wet, and waves from the rushing tide splattered us as we walked.

I invited everyone present to speak, but only *my* voice contributed to the ritual. My lines were prepared, and I didn't know if they were for Mike or for me. I read from *The Shoes of the Fisherman* by Morris West: "It takes so much to be a full human being that there are very few who have the enlightenment or the courage to pay the price. One has to abandon altogether the search for security and reach out to the risk of living with both arms. One has to embrace the world like a lover. One has to accept pain as a condition of existence. One has to court doubt and darkness as the cost of knowing. One needs a will stubborn in conflict, but apt always to total acceptance of every consequence of living and dying."

I continued with a passage from *The Sea Around Us* by Rachel Carson, a book Mike had been reading: "On all these shores there are echoes of past and future; of the flow of time, obliterating yet containing all that has gone before; of the sea's eternal rhythms, the tides, the beat of the surf, the pressing rivers of the currents, shaping, changing, dominating; of the stream of life, flowing as inexorably as any ocean current, from past to unknown future. For as the shore configuration changes with the flow of time, the pattern of life changes."

I held the creel by its straps. With everyone's eyes upon me, I opened the cover, removed the lid from the urn, and looked quickly at the gray powder inside. Nothing recognizable remained. I glanced at each member of my family, then reached back as far as I could, and heaved the creel into the hungry ocean. I watched in silence as my fisher-kid's powdered ashes were absorbed by the sea.

Kelli-Lynne interrupted my thoughts. "When are we going to have a picnic?" she wanted to know. "You said we could eat, and I'm hungry, and I want to play pirates."

"Right, Kelli-Lynne, I promised you could eat."

"Since it's my brother's birthday, why is everyone so quiet? And where is Mikey's birthday cake?"

For two weeks I had been preparing her, or at least I had thought so. Having regretted my decision to exclude her from the funeral, I considered her presence today especially important. As I walked to the picnic table with her, I mused over the similarities between Kelli-Lynne's life and Mike's death. The attention I give to Kelli-Lynne is external; my eyes, ears, and hands are open for her. The attention I give to Mike is internal. His absence makes as many demands on me as her presence. I resent Mike for dying, for demanding that I grieve. My grief separates me from Kelli-Lynne, then I resent her constant questioning because she distracts me from missing Mike. I have two demanding children—one living, one dead.

The picnic table was covered with food. Off to the side was a blueberry pie I baked yesterday. Because of the unfinished pie I was making the afternoon Mike died, I thought I'd never attempt another one. But I did, and I filled it with blueberries Mike had picked and left in the freezer.

Everyone was talking, and I didn't feel much like joining in. Then I spotted a man strolling by with a fishing rod. "Another fisherman," I said aloud.

Kelli-Lynne pulled at my coat, asking, "Mom, do you think Mikey will help that man catch fish?"

"I don't know. What do you think?"

"I think if Mikey likes him, he will. Now can I eat? And when will you play pirates with me, Mom? You *promised*."

"Now, Kelli-Lynne," I replied. As I walked toward the rocks with my daughter skipping ahead, I looked out at the water. There was no sign of Mike's creel or his ashes. All was waves and spray . . . and endless ocean.

May 7, 1977

*F*amiliar footsteps at the back door sparked the hope that Mike had come home. I thought jubilantly, He is alive after all! I rushed to open the door, only to greet three of Mike's classmates. I looked into their eyes and started to cry.

One boy was holding a large book. "We thought you would like to have Mike's yearbook," he said awkwardly.

Another explained, "We didn't know what to do, because we didn't know what you'd want, so we passed his yearbook around to his friends, and everyone signed it. I hope that's okay."

"Thank you," I said softly. I opened the book. All the autographs and captions were written in the present tense.

"What does 'T.F.F.' mean?" I asked as I paged through the inscriptions.

"True Friends Forever." His voice cracked.

I shook my head. I didn't know what to say, what to do. Kelli-Lynne burst into the room, excited to play with Mikey's friends.

"Mrs. Hall, I picked up Mike's letters for track and swimming," said the third boy. "I thought you might like to put them in his scrapbook."

My hands trembled as I accepted Mike's athletic emblems. How hard he had worked for them! Early in March I had bought yarn to knit a sweater for these letters, and only yesterday I tripped over the bag containing the yarn, which I had inadvertently buried under a stack of clothes.

I agreed to appear at a benefit dance the students were sponsoring in Mike's memory. His friends, wanting something to remind them of Mike, were planning to purchase a plaque to be emblazoned with each year's top student athlete—all of which was to be announced at the benefit.

I don't know how I can manage to appear at a dance in honor of Mike. I want to be gracious and let his classmates know how much I appreciate their thoughtfulness, but I don't know what to do with my pain. God, I thought I was beginning to heal, especially after getting through the final ritual on Mike's birthday. Now I feel raw and exposed.

May 12, 1977

I am absorbed with myself. I don't recall ever being this way before. Until recently, my attention has almost always been directed toward others. I wish I could slip under a microscope and see myself as a biologist would. No, that wouldn't work. So much of what I am these days is what I am feeling, and microscopes don't magnify feelings. Does it always take a crisis before one dares to look within?

June 15, 1977

I am anxious about returning to teach at CPSI next week. [See For More Information on page 197.] After four years there, a part of me yearns to go back and attempt to be who I was before my son's death, and another part is not ready to.

CPSI has been an oasis for my creative spirit. For one week each summer, I teach and learn and dare to be who I am becoming. Now, however, I live more with grief than with creativity, and I do not want to be reminded of Mike's death. I don't like leading with my grief and being so self-absorbed, but I have no other way.

June 23, 1977

Three months after Mike's death, I return to teach and be with the friends I see once a year. I sit alone on a high hill that has been dubbed "Rosie's mountain." So many people have approached me to offer their sympathies. I dread the reminders. I want people to acknowledge me for something else, *anything* else. No one here knew Mike, yet they know me now as the mother of a son who has died. And this was the year I'd planned to bring him here with me so he could be challenged intellectually and creatively. In fact, his name was on the register.

I want a vacation from grief. I want to be only Rosie. My laughter sounds hollow to me, and as I reflect on the day, I have to admit that it's awkward not knowing how to respond when people show genuine concern. Avoiding people and keeping busy have become my allies. I amaze myself when I act like my family.

June 28, 1977

$\mathcal{Y}$esterday I was frightened when a mortician who was sitting at my table in the CPSI cafeteria casually mentioned that 83 percent of married couples divorce after the sudden death of a child. I don't want to be a statistic. I want only to heal, so I've kept myself busy teaching, parenting, and drinking too much wine.

I don't know how to be real anymore. I smile a lot; I walk fast; and I avoid paying attention to my pain.

July 1, 1977

$\mathcal{T}$his week of teaching has passed too quickly. Why is it so difficult for me to receive support? I feel guilty about Mike's death, guilty about pretending that my life is in good order, and guilty to be alive when he is dead. Worst of all, I feel guilty about feeling guilty.

I go home tomorrow. For tonight, Bob and I have scheduled eight hours of work on our book. My mind seems to be in gear again. I can think. I can plan. I can design strategies to fit theories. My heart is buried, and I feel dismembered.

July 10, 1977

$\mathcal{W}$here would I be without Kelli-Lynne? She distracted me after Mike died, and I welcomed the diversion. Without her, I might have immersed myself in work, or divorced Gil, or given in to depression.

Children occupy my thoughts. I am jealous of my sister-in-law as she grows bigger in her pregnancy. My brother insists that if they have a son, he will be named after Mike. I argue with him, "It's too soon! I can't stand it!" I pray they have a daughter. I also have fleeting thoughts of adopting a child, but I know I would not stop missing Mike, or even allow the child to be who he is. Nor is ours a marriage that can nurture another child.

What replenishes me most of all is writing. When I write, I see myself more clearly and gradually forgive myself.

It's simple. You will when you will.

How clearly and easily the answers emerge, even when I don't know I've asked a question. It's as though a well deep inside spurts forth with an answer before I can blink. When I imagine where in my body the well might be, I sense it is in my heart.

Don't forget soul.

I feel incompetent, because nothing feels permanent. Even so, right here, right now, on the tenth of July, I affirm the importance of my heart. I believe that promise resides in my pain. I am willing to struggle. I do believe I am doing the best I can right now.

July 28, 1977

It's been three months since Mike's body was cremated. Will I be forever measuring my life in terms of my son's death?

A life is extinguished, but traces of it are everywhere. Closing Mike's bank account, for instance, was a nightmare. I walked into the bank remembering that I was seven years old the first time I opened an account there. Some of the tellers had seen me grow up. Did they know about Mike or would I have to tell them? I was relieved to see the woman who had opened my first account. "This will be easy," I whispered. "She'll understand."

"I want to close Mike's account," I said softly. I hoped I wouldn't have to tell her. I pleaded with my eyes, Don't ask me. She reached for a form and asked.

"Mike is dead," I said in a hollow voice. I turned away, wanting to run. "Forget the money," my mind shrieked. "Forget the bonds. Forget the paperwork. I don't know how to do this."

The teller excused herself. A man appeared and told me in an official tone of voice that I would need "proof of death" before the account could be closed and the funds transferred to my daughter's account. What better proof of death could there be than me?

"You'll need a death certificate before the paperwork can be done," he said calmly.

"You mean I have to come here *again?* Can't you take my word for it?"

"I'm sorry, ma'am, it's standard procedure."

Standard procedure. Since when is death standard procedure? To him I said, "I will get a death certificate, but can this be done through the mail? Coming here once is enough."

"Under normal circumstances, no, but—"

"Thanks," I said, almost knocking over the man behind me as I made my escape.

"Rosalie!" the man said, regaining his composure. "And how is my namesake?"

This can't be happening, I thought. I have just literally bumped into the doctor I named my son after! How could he not have known? At that moment I heard the teller call, "Dr. Mike." I flew through the words: "He is dead. He was electrocuted in my backyard four months ago."

Dr. Mike's face turned ashen. He reached out for me, but I ran out the door and all the way down Main Street to the beach. I didn't cry, for fear that someone might notice. But I was ashamed I hadn't conducted myself properly at the bank, and I did not want to have to look at my son's death certificate.

July 30, 1977

Peggy came to visit. On some days, like this one, Mike's death seems as recent as yesterday. Other days, it seems a lifetime away. When I had a skin, I didn't question time; now that it's been shed, time is new. Peggy understood all this. While grieving she, too, learned that time has no context.

We talked about the tension in my marriage. Peggy could feel it in the house. "I need to talk about Mike," I explained, "but Gil never mentions him. I hold back my tears because it isn't safe to be vulnerable with him, then I feel deprived and angry. I think we need help, but he refuses to see a counselor with me. 'This is between *us*,' he says. Seeing a counselor by myself would separate us even more, I think."

I looked at Peggy, then added, "I want to nurture and be nurtured in my marriage, and it's not happening." This was the first time I had dared to say the words out loud. Peggy told me I am encountering these experiences for the purpose of strengthening. I don't want to hear that. I want someone to tell me what to do. Right now.

Inner balance is the key.

Strength resides in gentleness.

Vision is a sensitive synthesis.

Once again, the answers appear. This is the connection: when I am receptive to myself, I hear the voice that springs from my depths. When

I yield, the flow begins, but when I pretend to be in control, I hear nothing. To achieve balance, I need both vulnerability and a new kind of strength.

July 31, 1977

Treating Kelli-Lynne and two of her girlfriends to a day at the fair drew me out of myself. I saw the world through the eyes of three year olds. I squealed with them during the greased pig scramble. I felt tender as we patted a newborn calf. We delighted in wandering without restrictions. No clocks, no schedules . . . only four girls at the fair.

I am looking forward to the upcoming training workshop in Gestalt therapy, which begins tomorrow. I'm going to stay in the dormitory, though I could easily commute the twenty miles from home. I want to concentrate on the training, walk on the beach, rest, and be released from family responsibilities. I've never been to a group-process workshop before. I plan to be very careful about letting people get too close to me. Two of my friends will be there; their protection is important, because I feel close to breaking down.

Breaking down is sometimes a prerequisite to breaking through.

I am afraid to break down, yet I desperately need to break through. This is a chance for me to be with people I don't know. They'll have no expectations of me, so I won't have to live up to the standards of others.

Accept. Take what is given freely. Strife is not integral to existence. Only when you reject, object, and project does struggle become connected with being.

Frustration is undigested satisfaction.

Believe in yourself, and all is possible. You are an instrument of light and power. You are prepared: only commitment and faith are needed to bring your gifts to fruition.

There are those around you who are afraid of what you are living. They will discourage you, yet your direction is charted. You are becoming a clear channel, and your motives are pure.

Know that you are protected. We are concentrating our energies on your evolution.

Who is "we"? What is my "direction"? What does it mean to be "an instrument of light and power"? I was just getting used to seeing sentences appear, and now paragraphs are emerging. Truly, I don't know what to do with information like this. How do I understand or talk about it? I can't say, "Before me is a paragraph I didn't write. I typed it, but I was not the source of the words."

The words just come—from where, I do not know. I pause, stop questioning, and take a deep breath. My heart fills with peace.

August 1, 1977

I am shaky here at the workshop. My two women friends canceled at the last minute. I feel alone and vulnerable, yet I realize it is perfect for me not to have friends to lean on this week.

During the morning group, I encountered more ambivalence. I wanted to watch and to rest. I also wanted to work. Finally, I said I was impatient for more interaction. The leader gently asked me, "What would you like to ask, and of whom?"

I looked around to a woman on the other side of the room and asked what issues she was working on. Another woman interrupted, demanding that I talk about what *I* wanted to work on. Without thinking, I said my fourteen-year-old son had been killed four and a half months ago. I quickly reassured everyone that I was dealing with his death and was in control. Glancing around the room, I noticed people with tears in their eyes. One man reached over to hold my hand.

The leader asked if I was aware that I smiled when I spoke about my pain.

"No," I replied.

Someone else observed that I switched my focus from speaking about my pain to searching the faces of those around me. Suddenly I realized that I must have been scanning their faces to distinguish between people caring for me and people feeling sorry for me. I didn't want anyone to take pity on me. I want honesty and depth from others, but I'm unwilling to let them see my pain. Mike's death is my depth now; all else is cocktail chatter. I don't want to be emotionally corseted, yet I don't know how to lower my guard in the presence of others.

At the end of the day, I relaxed by the water with two men. The conversation centered around the need to pay more attention to intuition. In talking, I discovered there is more to me now than my pain. My intuitive process is real to me.

Tonight the moon lights up my tiny room. I bathe in the brilliant white lunar light. I noticed on my way to the bathroom three spiderwebs spun in a three-dimensional design. When I am in a place that is right for me, there is always a spider's web. Spiders intrigue me. I think that if I could watch a spider weaving a web, I might understand more about life and death.

August 3, 1977

I awoke early, feeling energized and well rested despite few hours of sleep. During a break this morning, a workshop participant asked if I wanted help in grappling with Mike's death. Before I could respond, he offered to support me in my grief process. Grateful, I told him I didn't want to do this work in the large group because my grief felt too personal. What I longed to say was, "Don't you understand? In my family we grieve *alone.*"

We talked about timing. I told him I was sure we don't receive more than we are ready for. I sounded so knowledgeable. Where did it come from? I had no idea I carry so much within me.

As we headed back to the group, my friend commented, "You wouldn't have been given the gifts you have, or the experiences you've had, unless you were supposed to share them." He winked at me, saying, "There are no coincidences, you know."

August 5, 1977

*E*verything is woven together. I don't know how to celebrate my daughter's birthday without thinking of my son's death. Life and death are like twins. I chose to be at the Gestalt training workshop during Kelli-Lynne's third birthday so as to gain some distance between the joy I felt at her birth and my depression over Mike's death. I don't understand why I can't separate the two events.

A mother is a mother is a mother.

Today was the day of Kelli-Lynne's birthday party. As if to reinforce my inner conflict, I tripped over one of Mike's old sneakers while carrying her birthday cake down the back stairs. The sneaker had been wedged under the porch, but this was the first time I had seen it. In the act of tripping, I recalled how Mike had teased everyone at Kelli-Lynne's party last year. He had tried to eat all the cake and had made faces at the little kids. I could never understand why he acted out like this during family occasions.

Kelli-Lynne's eyes grew big when she saw what I held in my hands. She'd asked for a green panda bear cake, and after borrowing a mold I was able to surprise her with one. She and her friends squealed with happiness when I set the final masterpiece on the picnic table and lit the candles. Amid shouts of "I want an ear" and "I want the nose," I reminded Kelli-Lynne to make a wish.

While grateful that Kelli-Lynne was delighted with her cake, her presents, and her day, I was grieving the fact that I would never orchestrate another party for Mike. Why is it so difficult to celebrate the present? If I had my life to live over, I would ask for wisdom first, children second.

August 10, 1977

I remember with stunning clarity last night's dreams. In the first one I was riding a huge Ferris wheel. I was afraid of the heights as well as the sudden descents, but I forced myself to stay on board. To be on the Ferris wheel, I now see, is to *feel* something.

The second dream opened with a party scene. Mike was there, and I knew he was about to wrestle with an older person. The scuffle began in fun, but Mike got cornered and started punching in earnest. His opponent suddenly became younger than himself, and instead of admiring Mike's courage, I became angry at him for being a bully. People looked at me, and no one knew what to do. I approached Mike, and the fight stopped.

I said to him, aware that he was dead, "I haven't seen you in a long time. How are you?"

"Parts of me are dead," he answered, "and I was robbing you of life."

I tried to tell him he wasn't, but he faded out. I ran. Longing to hide, I escaped to the cellar, where I found fresh newsprint in a corner room. I needed to make sense of the mystery of Mike's death. Unprompted, I looked up to see a woman standing near me.

Suddenly the two of us were in a large room crowded with people. Women approached me, saying, "Your book was just what I needed," "How can I learn more from you?" and other similar comments.

When I woke up, I recalled how bonded I had felt to the child growing within me when I was one month pregnant with Mike. The integrity of that bond is what kept me from having an abortion; I had honored the spirit of the child I was carrying. After Mike was born, however, I lost my sense of that bond. I, who had fought so hard for his life, lacked a spiritual connection to him after his birth. Now, after his death, I again feel the preciousness of that intrauterine bond.

August 12, 1977

I am worried about Gil. He works too hard and falls into his separate bed every night about nine-thirty. He seldom talks to me about his feelings or about Mike. In his eyes I see pain; his voice and energy are monotonic.

Last night I watched him stare silently off into the distance, and I thought he might cry. I stayed unobtrusively quiet for about five minutes, then gently asked him what he was thinking.

"Nothing specific," he replied. "Lots of things."

"I'd be interested in hearing about any of them," I offered.

He suggested we have a glass of wine, and then asked about my day. I realized that as long as I talk, he doesn't have to. How do I help him talk about Mike without pushing?

Gil went to sleep in his room while I stayed alone in mine. Intuition told me an important dream was waiting for me, so I settled into sleep. I appeared radiant in the dream. My body glowed as if I had a sunburn, and I was interacting with someone who also shimmered with light; I couldn't tell if it was a man or a woman. The dream had no beginning or end, only images of radiance.

This morning when I woke up, I knew on an inner level that I had begun moving forward to embrace my radiance. I am radiant when I listen to my intuition. And I know, from the same place in my gut that took over with a psychic kick to further Mike's growth after death, that somehow he is a major part of this. Yet, his death continues to feel like a sacrifice to me.

A sacrifice for you.

Somehow I know that Mike's evolution and mine are linked. Maybe to the degree he evolves, I evolve. Do I dare assume that to the degree I evolve, *he* evolves, or am I being narcissistic? He told me there are no

separations, no divisions. Damn, why did my growing trust in my intuition have to be linked to his death?

Involvement leads to evolvement.

I am inspired when I am teaching. Part of what I am living and teaching is how to create different realities. I know I have more to live through
before I can teach with wisdom.

*Timing is not an accepted reality in our dimension. Look again. Can
you imagine that you chose to make the sacrifice by remaining in the
physical dimension? Death is not a sacrifice. Living is. You chose to
remain, to spin cobwebs.*

August 20, 1977

Another season is drawing to a close, and if Mike were alive, he would
be getting ready to enter his first year of high school. Summer vacation
was a reprieve: I didn't have to see the neighborhood kids leaving for
school each day. Even so, I felt raw, robbed of the fantasy that I was
dealing successfully with my loss. Seeing bikini-clad teenagers on the
beach, I would put on my sunglasses to hide my tears. Invariably, someone would recognize me and greet me, then we would both look quickly away. Others would ask if they could join me, or would offer to play
with Kelli-Lynne, or remark on how good I looked. No matter what they
said or didn't say, I wanted to put my sunglasses over my heart. Summer
could have been a transition time, yet here I sit, dreading the first day of
school. I feel as if I haven't passed into the next grade.

Apparently I didn't realize that I have expectations of myself. It's
been almost five months. How long will I carry on?

August 25, 1977

Last night in a dream, I was talking to my friend Carole. She said to me,
"You are really coming into your own power. I have seen this for a long
time. Intuition always has been your gift of prophecy."

I pleaded with her. "But how can I connect with Mike and help him
and myself at the same time?"

She looked at me, as if searching my mind. "What does your intuition say?"

"I am already doing it, but I need to hear someone else tell me that," I replied.

August 28, 1977

$\mathcal{I}$ am left with two fragments from last night's dreams. In one, I listened to a person reveal the secrets of being a wizard. In the other, I was able to see through a huge rock made of flawless mica. I tried to figure out if the transparency was caused by the light of the quartzlike crystal or by the way I was seeing. I woke up thinking, If I could see like that all the time, I would be a wizard.

Life is transparent to those who see.

The words appear on my paper.

Trust. Be with trust. Trust in being, and all will be transparent to you.

August 31, 1977

$\mathcal{A}$ neighbor visited this afternoon. She told me about her mother's difficult adjustment to menopause—her mood swings, nervousness, anxiety, and heart palpitations. After my neighbor left, I wondered if some of my low days were related to the hormonal changes my body has been going through since the hysterectomy. Pains in my chest sometimes run down both arms and may be symptomatic of hormonal famine. These pains scared me initially. I thought I was having a heart attack. Now when they occur, I concentrate on breathing, and eventually they disappear.

Daily, I swallow an estrogen pill. Hot flashes no longer plague me, but I detest taking the hormone. Ingesting estrogen implies that I am not in control of my body. Mike's death signifies that I am not in control of my life. No wonder my heart hurts!

Recently, I have been flooded with dreams. In the one I recall most vividly, I was in a bike race. The bike I was pedaling was built for three. I was in the middle position. My two companions and I pedaled hard uphill, but we made no progress. Suddenly I knew I should be sitting in the front seat. I demanded to take my rightful place, but a race official blocked my way, quoting from a rule book, "The lead man. . . ." I argued that "man" was used in the generic sense, but he objected.

Refusing to be squelched by an outdated rule book, I took the front seat despite his objections. My two teammates appeared uncertain of the realignment, but took their seats nevertheless. We shot forward and, because the distribution of power was balanced and natural, were able to move faster with no additional exertion. I was filled with confidence. As we pedaled closer to the top of the mountain, within sight of the winner's position, I realized I didn't know what was at the top of the mountain; I knew only that the race was important. The dream ended here. Nothing feels finished to me these days.

September 5, 1977

Today is the first day of school—a day I don't want to spend alone. While Gil was shaving this morning, I asked him to take the day off, but he refused. He advised me to pull down the shades to avoid seeing the kids on their way to school.

"But I want us to be together," I said in a shaky voice.

"That's impossible," he replied, shutting the bathroom door.

I started to cry. Then Kelli-Lynne tugged at my bathrobe, asking if I would play with her, and I agreed. So after breakfast, she and I escaped to Two Lights. Watching Kelli-Lynne scamper over the rocks while hunting for treasures, I felt less panicky. She would bend over, staring intently into tidal pools, gesturing in the same ways as her brother. I wondered how they would have gotten along, and what he would have been like this autumn. The inside of my face felt wet with tears, while I strained to keep from crying on the outside.

I looked to the ocean for solace, but found no comfort in the waves. There came instead a stirring to action, so I reached into my purse, took out a blank book, and wrote the following poem:

Mike's Legacy

The pain of letting go pierces my pulse
As my heart contracts and spurts spasms of fear
And my eyes reflect an arid expression,
The aftermath of uncried tears.

Echoes of unanswered questions and words of love
Left unsaid; ceaseless activity betrays my desperate attempts
To disengage. Not even night brings comfort
To assuage the ebb and flow of timeless memories.

Slowly, and with subtlety, I mutely attempt the descent
To open the center where my wounded heart
Feels spent. And once again, I am reunited with
The anguish of Instant Eternity—
His, not mine.

Without warning, my vision expands
And the moment of awareness
Between the grief and the promise that was-to-be
Emerges in a sea of acceptance
Wonder and mystery
As I realize
If it were not for him, I would not be me.

As I wrote the last word, I looked up and watched the effortless sweep of the waves into the exposed crevices of rock. Each wave was different. Some thundered and belched forth seaweed; others made not even a splash. Water transforms, I observed. My tears tasted of salt. Do tears, too, have the power of transformation?

Within you are gravitation pulls. Dare to feel your own tides.

I closed my book, waved to Kelli-Lynne, scaled the rocks, and invited her to play pirates with me.

September 9, 1977

Here's another example of how I set myself up. Yesterday, with the entire family gathered together at my parents' camp, I imagined we would find time to talk about Mike and how we were coming to terms with his death. Nobody mentioned his name, which only heightened my sense of his absence. In the morning my mother and I wandered from garage sale to garage sale, but we did not speak. Some of the adults spent the afternoon playing cards, while I watched Kelli-Lynne and her cousin Travis romp in the sun. Gil slept. None of the adults talked; in fact, we were seldom in the same room at the same time. As I started to tell my parents how difficult the first day of school had been for me, someone switched on the television set.

That night a dream highlighted my reality. I was at a zoo, looking at a caged human being. She was always smiling. I watched for a long time, then got bored. I began to make faces, hoping to trick the captive into responding to me, but she only copied me. I want so much to help this person experience more than a smile. I woke up sobered. It's getting harder for me to run from truth.

September 12, 1977

My calendar fills with professional commitments and personal dates. I feel crowded. Too much of my time is already spent. I wonder, Is this what I want to be doing?

Mike once coined the term "wasting." Sitting was wasting. Meditation was wasting. Daydreaming was wasting. He and I shared the notion that wasting was not allowed. "Busyness" seemed the opposite of wasting, but now I suspect that being busy can be wasting, too.

So many things about Mike remain a mystery to me. He used to watch the boy across the street, all the while taking notes on what he did and what time it was when he did it. I found firecrackers hidden in Mike's clock radio. One night, he shot BBs out his bedroom window and let someone else take the blame for it. Last December, his negativity soared; not knowing how to help him release his anger, I simply protected myself from him.

September 16, 1977

*M*y den has become a battlefield. Kelli-Lynne opens the desk drawers and stuffs her things inside, scribbles on any paper in sight, and drops her toys without picking them up. Giving her a desk drawer of her own hasn't worked, and I've run out of patience. I would hate to punish Kelli-Lynne or take measures that may inadvertently snuff out her spirit, so instead I grit my teeth.

I have been holding myself hostage as a parent since Mike's death. I want to be a perfect parent, and subconsciously I believe Kelli-Lynne's life depends on my discovery of the perfect way to discipline her. This is a twisted view of parenting.

Purple bumps dot my arms and legs. "Nerves," I mumble. Today, with some modicum of shame, I told my parents that I'm depressed. I actually used the word. "All I want to do is sleep," I said.

Dad told me he is upset that I am not managing. Mom quickly volunteered to take Kelli-Lynne for a while. "That won't solve the problem," I said. Although I do not know what will, at least I'm no longer pretending.

One of the ways I depress myself is by dwelling on the future. Already I'm thinking of how meaningless Christmas will be without Mike. Talking about him with my family would help, but nobody wants to listen. I imagine that they will try too hard to be filled with the Christmas spirit, and Mike's name will not be mentioned. The ornaments he made last year, however, will dangle from their trees, and he will be present in his absence. Sometimes it's easier to get sick than to try to change a family system.

I am loyal to the night and my dreams. Having had little luck in piecing together a sense of wholeness in my waking life, I look to night visions for my direction and integrity. My survival lies in my unconscious.

September 20, 1977

*W*hat luxury—two free mornings in a row while Kelli-Lynne is at play group. This morning Bill called. Newly separated, he wasn't at home to see his daughters on their first day of school. I listened and understood. Separations, like deaths, disrupt unity and continuity. Bill is having a long-distance love affair with his daughters, and I am having an urge to be in love with an idea, a project, a person. I am not in love with Gil, though I try to be. I want to be part of a family, and I want to feel love and be loved. Is there enough for me here? Is Gil enough?

Not now.

November 8, 1977

A friend called to tell me about a couple he knows whose nine-year-old son was killed by a truck while riding his bicycle. I sent a card to the couple, saying I, too, was a survivor. I offered my support and included my telephone number. The mother called. I encouraged her to do whatever she felt was right. As I confirmed, with a quivering voice, that she was now different from all her friends, our tears mingled over the telephone.

She said, "Nobody understands, and words seem hollow rather than comforting."

"Yes, I know," I told her.

And she knew I knew. We agreed to meet for lunch later in the week. And although I have no idea what she looks like, I know I will recognize her. An aura of pain surrounds a surviving mother.

After I hung up, I cried for her, for me, for all the mothers of the future who will experience the death of a child. I was exhausted from crying, but I felt a spark of satisfaction. I had used my experience to help someone in pain.

November 11, 1977

I had my first psychic reading today. The psychic used a regular deck of cards, and she started by saying I have intuitive knowledge. I will always be relationship oriented, but emotion is my Achilles' heel because I fear rejection. I sighed, thinking of Mike's death as the ultimate rejection.

"Do you have a son?" she asked.

"Yes," I said quietly.

"There is a strong spiritual connection between the two of you. A spiritual awakening awaits your relationship. The two of you have strong convictions, and your relationship alters the way you understand tragic events and happy events. For example, your relationship will change the way you deal with death."

I exhaled, unaware that I had been holding my breath. "My son died in March," I told her.

"You will never again view death as something that takes a person away from you, because you realize this is not the way it is. You will have periods of time in the next year when you will feel him around you. He may come to you in dreams, and tell you about things he is learning and where he is. Never doubt these dreams, because they are real."

I felt a bit anxious as she began leading up to my resolution cards. "You have the ace of hearts here, and that is the card of intense feelings. It's as though you have a big box of energy, love, emotion, and pain, and you have your thumb over the hole in the cover. In order to maintain your mental balance, you have to do that right now. It is not the time to tamper with your emotions. You will deal with the intense feelings, but not now."

I sighed. What a fury I had to look forward to!

"As for your resolution cards . . . do you have a daughter?"

"Yes," I replied.

"Your cards going into the future are somewhat unsettled."

I held my breath again, afraid she would tell me Kelli-Lynne was going to die. I resisted the urge to get up and run away.

"Your little girl is very psychic. She slips out of body frequently. She is an emotionally volatile person, and an open channel for her brother. Another thing I want to tell you is that you will love each other very much, but your relationship will be like that of best friends. The older she gets, the more intense your friendship will become."

It's odd that I haven't really felt like a mother to either of my children. With Mike, I felt like a sister, and we battled like siblings. With Kelli-Lynne, I feel like a friend and teacher.

The psychic continued. "Around Christmas, you are going to be missing your son, and you are going to go through the grief all over again. This time you will deal with it. The spiritual support you have awakened within you has been your strength, but the mother in you has not dealt with the loss of her child. The reality of his death will hit once again. You may very well feel your son around during this time, and he will be present. He will wait for you so that he can let go.

"Your little girl will bring you out of your depression. You will find her saying things about him or having dreams about him, and she will give you the emotional support you need. You will sense the three of you together. At that moment, you will have the emotional realization that you really are still a unit, but it is hell to go through.

"Now, about your son . . . he shows up in your resolution cards as pure spirit. He is leading you on to a highly spiritual place. He is free to grow and develop. I assume you have no worries about him. He is aspected so well."

"No, I don't worry about him. I have sensed his presence more this past month than right after his death."

"Oh, yes, because right after a person's death, there is always a shock. Your channels weren't open, and neither were his."

"I believe that whatever he is doing or learning is right for him," I said with conviction.

"It must be comforting to know you are entertaining a spark of energy very much like your own."

My ears perked up. "That's interesting. The understanding I received was that it didn't really make a difference who died—me or Mike— because we share a similar energy. The reason he died was that he was capable of maintaining our connection."

"Oh, he will keep the connection open. And in the future, you will find times when he is working with you, and then he will take off to do other things. Did someone tell you that it didn't matter who died?"

"I got it in a dream," I said quickly.

"That's good. It's reassuring. Once you get over this human part of your grief, your progress is tremendous."

November 14, 1977

*C*hange abounds. Eight months have passed since Mike died, and nothing is the same except his death. And yet, that is changing, too. At times, I feel close to him and sense his energy. Other times, I remember him but don't feel his presence.

I am in a quiet crisis without anchors. My career feels transitory; I used to love teaching, but I don't anymore. I used to enjoy being married and thought of families as support systems that pull together in a crisis, but my family has drifted apart. "We are all we need" has been my family's motto for as long as I can remember, and yet I need more. I wanted to believe in "Happily ever after," but my experience is, "They all died by degrees." I want to snuggle up to life instead of being frozen by death.

I'm reminded almost daily that intensity cannot be isolated. The intensity I feel in my depression is so pervasive that I've lost my sense of humor. I resent how hard I am working at all of this. If I could believe that change has a rhythm, I would relax and stop trying to control everything. If I were able to flow with universal rhythms, I would be more receptive to this process of change. Maybe the answer is, Once I believe it, I will see it. I giggle and add, Until that, too, changes.

November 23, 1977

In a dream I had last night, Mike was confined to an institution for the mentally disabled. He could not move or speak. I hated to see him reduced to a body with neither a mind nor vitality, and I felt guilty about my repulsion. I forced myself to visit him once a week, at which time I would speak to him, stare at him, and search for a sign that he heard me. He remained immobile, and I was horrified. How could this have happened to such an energetic person? I asked myself. In the midst of my agony, I heard Mike's voice saying, "You see, Mom, there are worse things in life than death."

I awoke suddenly, the sound of Mike's voice reverberating in my ears. Was I dreaming? Immediately I recalled the doctor at the hospital who had told me Mike was dead. He said that had Mike lived, he would have had to be institutionalized for the rest of his life. Eight months later, I am beginning to understand the horror we would have faced had he survived.

I sighed, put another blanket on the bed, and mused with resignation, Yes, there are worse things in life than death. But damn it, Mike, why?

"Don't you understand yet, Mom? I am a light."

His voice again, and this time I was awake.

"The question is, Do you believe in me? In yourself?"

I can't believe this, I told myself. I'm having a verbal conversation with my son whom I can no longer see or touch!

"Do you dare to believe? Dare to trust? Do you dare to see through?"

What does that mean? How is it possible to see through? See through *what?* I questioned.

"Rest. And trust in your senses."

I sighed again. What choice do I have?

"Revolving, involving, resolving, evolving—all is in process."

What kind of answer is that? I want something I can hold on to, I demanded.

There was only silence.

November 24, 1977

Last night's dreams are still with me. In one, I was a passenger on a luxury ocean liner, with no idea of our destination. Many of the people aboard were acquaintances, and I was surrounded by celebration. Mike was there, too. People asked me if we were still friends. The question of the day was, "Have you renewed your relationship?"

I woke up sensing that Mike is part of my present and my future. When I explained this to him, he said simply, "All is well." He added that once we begin to "invigorate" each other, I will know all is well.

In the second dream, I came upon a bloody car accident. People murmured that one driver was already dead, and there was no hope for the other. I bent down and cradled the dead man's head in my arms. He showed no vital signs, but I knew my presence was healing to him. Mike beckoned to me from the side of the road, inviting me to join him and others in celebration of "the dance." I refused, saying, "I can't be a part of your world. I need to be here. Someone is suffering, and I can help." Others left to join the dance, but I remained, cradling the stranger who was dead.

In the third dream, I was in the hospital giving birth. The baby boy weighed eight pounds eleven ounces. I awoke confused because I could not remember if I was the mother or the newborn. I am *still* confused.

It's all the same. There are no separations.

"But I'm a woman, so I should be giving birth to myself as a *girl*," I protest.

Souls have no gender—only essence.

November 27, 1977

Last night I talked with Gil about my depression. He listened and tried to understand. I asked him to go away with me for a weekend; I felt like I was begging. He refused to take a weekend away without Kelli-Lynne. He gives me everything but himself and time.

November 28, 1977

*M*y dreams have opened up in a way I don't understand. How do I bring their messages into my waking life? Or am I trying to do it backward? Is Mike delivering dreams to me?

In last night's dream, Mike's voice called me downstairs to the basement. When I was halfway down, he said, "Mom, I'm really glad you remembered to say I was a fisherman when you scattered my ashes."

After reaching the basement, I watched Mike at work on a beautiful boat. "It's for the family, for Christmas," he said with pride. "I've worked on the design for a long time."

I asked, "Will it fit through the cellar door?"

"Oh, Mom, of course. I told you—I think ahead now." And we both smiled.

The telephone woke me up. "This is Commander Flynn at the coast guard base. I'm sorry to bother you, ma'am, but do you have a son named Mike Hall?"

"Yes," I said softly.

"I would like to speak with him," said the official.

I looked around the bedroom, wondering, Am I awake or caught in a dream? "That's impossible," I stammered. "Mike is dead. He's been dead for eight months." Then I started to cry. "Hello," I said, shaking and confused.

"Yes, ma'am, I'm very sorry. I didn't know. But a boat was recovered last night, and the only identification on it were five lobster traps that had your son's numbers on them."

"There must be some mistake. Mike was building a boat, but it wasn't finished." No, that was in the dream, I remembered. Am I caught in the dream again? "Mike did have a lobster license," I said, "and he set fourteen traps out at my parents' camp two summers ago, but he didn't own a boat. He was only fourteen years old."

"I'm really sorry to bother you about all this, ma'am, but we're trying to locate the owner of the beached boat. The matter is under investigation. Thank you, Mrs. Hall. I'll write up the report. Good day."

Baffled and numb, I hung up the telephone. Questions surfaced: What is going on? Did a real telephone call interrupt my dream of Mike and his boat?

The phone rang again. It was my friend Marge. "Rosie I've been trying to get you for fifteen minutes, and your line was busy. Quite a conversation you had."

I hadn't made it up! If the line was busy, I reasoned, then that phone call was *real.*

"Oh, Marge, I don't know what to do," I moaned. Without hesitating I told her about my conversation with the coast guard commander.

"Have you called Gil?" Marge asked.

"He's at work, but I could try."

Gil wasn't available, so I left a message for him to call me. I waited until lunchtime to tell him. He listened quietly.

"I don't know why you're so upset, Rose. It was just a mix-up."

"But don't you think it's strange that the call came right after my dream, Gil?"

"Strange things happen, Rose."

"But what about—"

"Look, Rose, I have to get back to work early. If you want more information, call the coast guard."

I watched him leave. I felt as alone as I had in the hospital, upon learning of Mike's death. Then I dialed the coast guard and asked for Commander Flynn.

"Oh, yes, Mrs. Hall. The case is closed," the commander said. "Your son has been cleared, and the persons responsible have been apprehended by the authorities."

I sat down. "Cleared of *what?*"

"Smuggling drugs. Apparently the men read about your son's death and used his name to license their boat."

I cried, set down the phone, ran to the bathroom, and vomited. "How could anyone do that?" I screamed, and then vomited again. I splashed cold water on my face, and suddenly remembered I hadn't said good-bye to the commander. I picked up the receiver, but the line was disconnected. Apparently he had hung up.

November 29, 1977

*Y*esterday I had lunch with Ilene, the woman whose son was killed five weeks ago. It was easy to feel close to her because of our common experience. We spoke candidly about how cremation felt right for our sons, how "out of sync" we felt inside, and our ambivalent feelings about celebrating Christmas. We both admitted that if it weren't for our young daughters, we would skip the season altogether. The moment we began to confess how connected we felt to our sons' energies, the song "Lady, Are You Crying?" played on the overhead sound system. With tears pouring down our faces, we listened closely to the words: "Although I am not here, I am never closer to you than I am right now." I wanted to dismiss the timing and message of the song as coincidence, but I couldn't.

Meeting with Ilene enabled me to see how far I have come and how much further I have to go. We are two weeping mothers who are healing. As I write, I feel a stabbing pain in my chest, which I know is caused by my deep longing for Mike. This time, I breathe deeply and listen for the counsel of my inner voice.

Your heart chakra is opening. It is customary to close down to avoid the pain, but you are beginning to open to love. Your openings will be gradual, as long as you do not resist.

I think I understand. If I could feel more love, maybe I would feel less pain. Perhaps if I tried to talk more with Gil, I would feel closer to him.

You can have anything you want, as long as you are willing to let go.

The words dance in my head. If I let go of my expectation that Gil will share with me, will I then have what I want?

December 4, 1977

I've made some decisions. I don't enjoy teaching the psychology class, so I'm not going to renew my contract after the final session next week. Although it's scary not knowing how to replace my salary, I'm more afraid of losing enthusiasm for teaching by continuing to force myself to teach unwilling students.

My friend Alison called from Florida, asking me to lead a journal-keeping workshop in January. It would be a perfect time to escape the frigid weather, so I agreed. I've never been to Florida, and being paid to lead a workshop while spending time with Alison seems like a double miracle. Sunshine will be a bonus.

December 20, 1977

$\mathcal{I}$'m catching on: when I don't want to face myself, I don't write. If I don't see my pain on paper, I am able to deny it.

A small Christmas tree is now decorated and on the porch. If it were not for Kelli-Lynne, there would be no tree. She insisted on getting one, and on decorating it with shells, sand dollars, and starfish—all gifts from the sea, collected by Mike. While hanging the last of the aquatic ornaments, I started to feel Kelli-Lynne's excitement. We went on to string cranberries, weave the finished strands over the branches, and set red satin balls in place. Gazing at the fully adorned tree, I saw it as a symbol of the past as well as the present.

At a small pre-Christmas gathering, one of Gil's friends griped about the behavior of his teenage son. I left the room because I began to feel an unbearable yearning for Mike. What's the best way to respond when parents complain about their teenagers? Do I excuse myself politely? Do I ask them to stop? Acquaintances either forget that my son is dead or don't know that I'm still grieving. I want to bellow, "Ease up. Your sons and daughters are alive. Hold them before it is too late."

December 21, 1977

$\mathcal{I}$ woke up feeling tired and didn't want to get out of bed. I snapped at Kelli-Lynne several times, only because I wanted to be left alone. A book about hope rested on the couch where I had left it last night—a reminder that I was still depressed.

When Gil came home for lunch, I admitted that I was worn out and asked if he would take the rest of the day off so he could watch Kelli-Lynne while I rested. He shrugged his shoulders, spelled out five ways in which I was being unreasonable, and said that this was a depressing season for everybody. I felt like a victim. Are victims the same as martyrs?

Gil suggested that I ask my mother to come stay with Kelli-Lynne. I nixed the idea because the roads were icy and I didn't want my mother to see me depressed. I imagined she would lecture me about doing too much for too many, then she would bounce around my house whistling, singing, and appearing cheerful. I have no tolerance for pretense.

Am I the only family member still devastated by Mike's death? Here we are, embarking on the first Christmas without him, and everyone acts as if nothing has changed. I don't know how to manage missing him when I'm the only one feeling depressed.

Eventually Kelli-Lynne took a nap, and I took a tranquilizer, the first since Mike's death—and the last, I promised myself. Thinking about all the things I needed to do, however, kept me from sleeping. Soon Kelli-Lynne got up, and I started to cry. I told her I was sorry to have been so hard on her, but I missed Mike. She looked at me for a long time, then jumped onto my lap and hugged me, whispering, "I miss my brother, too." I rocked us.

Evening set in. I resigned from cooking supper. I resigned from being a mother. A friend came to visit, and I heard Gil say I was "courting the flu." Flu is permissible; depression, clearly, is not. Where do I turn from here?

December 22, 1977

*G*il surprised me by wandering into my bedroom tonight. I was distracted, studying the ceiling. Actually I was looking directly through it to the night sky. The boundary of "ceiling" had disappeared! The scintillating energy of the starry sky pulled on me, and I felt like I was having an orgasm.

I nudged Gil, saying, "Check out the ceiling," but all he saw was white paint. I told him what I was seeing. He groaned. Then Kelli-Lynne woke up, and he left to rearrange her covers. I knew he would not return.

I focused on the night sky in my room, hypnotized and anxious, as if my whole body had been awaiting this experience for a long time. My pulse accelerated. I wanted to know all there was to know. I took a deep breath and said out loud, "I am ready."

Silver and gold streams of light filled the room. As I watched, I could see each particle of light both separately and as part of a stream. My eyes felt like the shutter of a sophisticated camera. The streams of silver and gold coalesced, blanketing my heart. As they did, the light turned white. My body was light; I was light. I was not out of my body, but rather *in the light*.

Suddenly I sensed a familiar energy. I looked up, expecting to see a ghost. Instead, I was captivated by a swirl of light with a revolving center. I recognized this familiar, loving energy as Mike. Then I sensed Mike's voice—not in my ears, but rather in each cell of my body.

"That's right," he said. "I am sending you the essence of love, which is light. I can do that now."

As I watched even more intently, I noticed tiny rays of white light emanating from my heart and joining the energy spiral that was Mike. I wasn't trying to *do* anything; the convergence simply happened. I transmitted my thought: "I don't understand this."

"Just relax. Be with the light. You are experiencing that you, too, can send light."

"But my streams of light are nothing compared with yours," I complained.

"That's because you have not yet let go. You must release fully the emotion you have invested in me. Only then can we begin the transfusion."

"How do I let go?" I questioned.

"By blessing my passage. You released my body in the hospital, but what is needed now is a deeper release—for by blessing my evolution, you bless your choice to remain here as an instrument of healing. And within healing, we mutually evolve. You see, our souls' evolution is connected, and to reinvest in the light, you must bless my choice of evolution."

"I can't bless your death," I told Mike.

"'Death' is your word," he reminded me. "I am living energy. I have motion and intention. If I had left for college or married, you would have given me your blessing. Both of us would have experienced a new beginning, further learnings, a different relationship."

"But that time was far away," I complained. "College was three years in the future; and marriage, many years. I can't make that jump."

"Time is all relative. Past, present, future—all are 'now' in my dimension," Mike told me.

His words of wisdom reminded me that our ages no longer mattered, either. Our realities had become so different. I was not relating to the son I had birthed and raised.

"Your blessings are a vote of confidence in our mutual evolution. You are experiencing the resonant vibrations that connect us. The radiant energy that you are impressed with can be received and channeled on a daily basis, but only after you have released me from your heart."

"In other words, it is my function to disconnect . . . again," I said.

"Precisely," he responded. "There are levels of releasing, depths of letting go. You have now glimpsed an aspect of your own radiance, but you must be willing to release me. I cannot do that for you. That is your learning and your work. Know that in letting go you will experience light. Trust in your own radiance. Trust in our magnetic radiance."

"Why me? Why do you 'appear' to me. Why am I the one to let you go?"

"I visit with those who are receptive. I am a beginner. It takes concentrated study to master the laws of transforming energy, and I manifest to those who are most receptive, trusting you will carry my messages to others.

"Tomorrow, ask Dad to join you at Two Lights. I will give you a sign that you will recognize. Trust that Dad will know where to go and what to say. He will have no idea where his words are coming from, or what effect they have on you. Just as you are losing all faith about the reality of my visit, I will manifest light. Remember, once I was your son, and I shall manifest a sun sign for you. It is our covenant. Truth resides within the light. Trust life.

"Rest now, Mom, for it *will* be a merry Christmas."

I felt our unity. With no qualms, I said aloud, "I release you, Michael, my son. I bless your spirit. I bless your life, and I release you."

Immediately, I felt crowned with energy. My mind and my heart were one. Everything seemed so obvious, including my visits to Two Lights. I laughed out loud, realizing with every ounce of my being that Mike and I *are* two lights. The concept of no divisions was becoming clear. I am understanding a different reality.

December 23, 1977

*O*n the twenty-third day of every month I relive the death of my son, and this one marked the day to go to Two Lights with Gil. We walked in silence down the winding road to the park. I felt alone, but not lonely. A gentle inner strength flowed through me.

The sky was a mass of large clouds that left not a trace of blue. I thought, No way will light ever break through this grayness. Yet, the immensity of the love I felt in my heart reminded me of Mike's promise. I had done my part; I had let go. Now what?

I followed as Gil walked with deliberation to a high bluff overlooking the ocean. Quietly, as if to himself, he said he was content with our decision to scatter Mike's ashes here. "Now Mike is a part of the ocean and a part of the universe," he explained.

The sun appeared, and I began laughing and crying, one after the other. I felt as if a huge weight had been lifted off my shoulders.

Gil looked blank, unable to fully appreciate my excitement. I knew that Christmas would be okay, that I would be okay, and that I would be able to welcome my brother's baby without feeling guilty, selfish, or immersed in grief.

December 24, 1977

I returned to the neighborhood beach with Kelli-Lynne and my nephew Travis. There we were, reveling in fifty-degree weather! We stripped off our coats, and the kids made a sand birthday cake for Baby Jesus. We collected shells, snails, seaweed, and sea grass for cake decorations. We sang "Happy Birthday," and the kids followed up with Christmas carols.

Kelli-Lynne asked if I would show her how to do a cartwheel, so I jumped up, spread my hands and legs, and windmilled through the air. I turned one cartwheel after another to the water's edge as the kids clapped with glee. When I flopped down in the mud, they gathered around me and we rolled over one another, laughing with delight. For a short time, I was free—unencumbered by judgment and relishing my life.

When we got back to the house, the kids raced around, paying no attention to the brightly wrapped packages under the tree. We had to coax them to sit down and receive their gifts. With the arrival of my parents and grandmother, Kelli-Lynne gathered up ribbon, tinsel, and paper, and taped ornaments all over her small body. She danced around the living room, falling over rolls of paper and stacks of opened boxes, conscious only of her "treeness."

Mom handed me a gift, saying she hoped I liked it. I unwrapped the green and red paper cautiously. She had embroidered my poem "Mike's Legacy." I cried. Everyone looked away. Reading the words over to myself, I thought, Yes, I am finally passing through resignation to renewal.

Mom's voice called me back to reality. Now, instead of being angry and hurt that no one had mentioned Mike, I accepted the silence. For the time being, it was enough to miss him.

Gil and I went off to a full moon meditation, picking up friends along the way. I needed so much to feel the sacredness of Christmas; being with the family, opening presents, drinking eggnog, and hearing the music in the background had failed to fill me up. During the silent meditation, I saw visions of sculpted stained-glass windows and two hands clasped in prayer.

We went on to a Christmas Eve candlelight service, which was disappointing . My soul yearned to be feasted with music, but the choir was off-key. I tried to concentrate on the candles and the incense, but the magic was dispelled by chattering teenagers sitting directly behind us. This was the first time I'd been in a church since Mike's death, and church, I decided, didn't seem to be my medium.

The vastness you are in search of is within. You are the mystery. You are the magic. You bring to yourself candles and incense, and an open heart and mind.

December 25, 1977

Christmas morning, and Gil and I stayed in bed until nine o'clock. I was amazed that Kelli-Lynne managed to sleep so late when her stocking and presents were under the tree, waiting to be opened.

We ended up celebrating Christmas three times this year: yesterday with my family, at home this morning with the three of us, and later in the day with Gil's family. On the two-hour drive to their house, we sang Christmas carols. We also talked about the upcoming birth, for my sister-in-law was in labor. As if on cue, Kelli-Lynne asked questions about her brother: What did I think Mikey was doing to celebrate Christmas? Would he have a stocking? Would the new baby know Mikey had died? What did I think Mikey would do if he were riding in the car with us now? How could she wish him a Merry Christmas? Would he hear her? She didn't wait for answers.

Later in the day, Kelli-Lynne left everyone speechless when she casually dialed a number on her new toy telephone, told Mikey she really missed him, and wished him a Merry Christmas. She then asked everyone in the room to talk to her brother so he would know we *all* still loved him. I marvel at how she takes care of herself.

I retreated early to bed with Kelli-Lynne. We whispered together, and for about two hours I smoothed her back and shoulders. With her I feel my sacredness.

Disappearing into my own room, I fell asleep instantly and later awoke to the moon's light. Filled with a sense of wonder, I crept out of bed, covered myself with the quilt, and gazed out the window. Snow blanketed the ground, and the ice on the lake shimmered in the moonlight. The nocturnal world was alive with white light, and I simply watched it all with reverence.

After a while the telephone rang, and my sister-in-law announced that I was an aunt to a niece. I was delighted and relieved. There was no way they would name a daughter Mike!

December 26, 1977

Christmas is over—the celebrations and special treats, the travel, the *mess*. Now our world can return to normal. I stopped by the hospital to welcome my new niece, Ellenor Ann. She is so tiny, and her head is shaped like Kelli-Lynne's. As I inspected her through the glass partition, hard as I tried, I could not picture my own children as infants. What happens to those images? How can early bonding memories vanish so quickly?

I wondered if I would remember how to hold a newborn. I am focusing on birth and growth once again, I realized. Death and grief have held me captive for too long.

My dream life exploded this past week. It is like an undercurrent that shapes the contours of my life. My truth will probably continue to reside within the darkness of night until I am able to dream my way into the light.

In what announced itself as "the return dream," I saw the word *return* in seven consecutive scenes, each of which focused on my past. The first scene was set in high school. Wearing tight skirts and boasting a full bosom, I was busy searching and very lonely. Then came a composite of Rainbow Assem-blies in which I was elected Worthy Advisor and was proud to receive this top honor, but still aware that something was missing. The third scene involved my romance with Andy and the beginning of my sexual life; then came images of Mike's birth. The fifth revealed me attending college, meeting Gil, and pretending nothing was missing. Next came Mike's death: he was alone, and I was missing. The seventh scene I no longer remember.

When I woke up I said to myself, "All this has passed. It is time to reinvest." I sensed that Mike was behind each of the scenes.

In another dream, Gil and I were in Montreal, heading for a ship that was anchored in the harbor. With me in the lead, we slowly inched our way over a ribbonlike bridge that was very close to the water. At points along the bridge were handles we could latch on to; other places offered no means of support. Walking was impossible because the passage was too narrow, so we moved forward in a seated position. I was cold, and every once in a while a wave splashed over onto me. Looking down into the water scared me, so I concentrated on facing directly ahead and keeping the ship in view. Gil and I did not talk.

Suddenly, the narrow bridge arched, presenting a twisted curve that seemed impossible to negotiate. Just as I was ready to give up, a voice within chided: "You can do it. You *must* do it. In your own way. Your destination is in sight." I took a deep breath and looked back at Gil. He shrugged his shoulders. I returned my gaze to the ship and with renewed determination, slowly mounted the curve. Much to my delight, I discovered that I could slide effortlessly down the inside part of it. Tumbling into the water seemed less scary now, because I knew I could swim.

A man appeared and asked us what we were doing. When I told him, he pointed to another bridge—the "traffic bridge." I told him I hadn't seen it, and besides, it wouldn't take me where I wanted to go.

"No," he said, "it will take you to the gift shop." He explained that the route to the ship was not charted and could not be bridged through normal channels. I was determined to go on. I glanced back at Gil, wondering if he would continue with me. He told me he was glad we were together for this adventure, but he was finished. I nodded and resolved to go on alone. I woke up before reaching the ship.

December 30, 1977

*G*il and I are drifting farther apart. He putters around the cellar while I write. We make no demands on each other. To practice being a couple, I asked him to go cross-country skiing with me. I was surprised when he accepted. Then an hour before the babysitter was due, he told me he would rather stay home with Kelli-Lynne.

Setting off for the snowy woods, I recalled the time Mike and I had skied together last winter. I remembered the smile he gave me each time I tried to get back on my feet after a fall. Now I was skiing again, alone and pregnant with memories.

Wrapped in a scarf, thermal mittens, and a woolen hat, I slowly traced someone's trail, all the while recounting childhood messages of defeat: "You aren't coordinated," "Your ankles aren't strong enough," "You're not graceful." I froze at the thought of skiing down a hill, even a small one.

"I can. I *can*," I shouted into the icy stillness.

Suddenly I realized that while wandering through my memories, I had forgotten what I was doing; instead of mechanically telling myself to slide one foot in front of the other, I was simply gliding along. The sun's reflection on the fresh snow created sparks of light. The land sprawled in places, flattened out, then regained its three-dimensionality. The silence of the woods eradicated all self-consciousness, and I moved toward stillness and beauty with coordinated grace.

The dream I had last night was somewhat similar. I was visiting someone in jail when suddenly I didn't know which side of the bars I was on. A dancer came in and performed, which confused me more. Was I the visitor, the prisoner, or the dancer? As the dream ended, I realized that only the dance was real.

December 31, 1977

I have survived The Year That Mike Died. I have survived the year I turned thirty-three years old. Someone once told me that in the thirty-third year, one chooses to either live or die. Perhaps it is true.

This morning I bumped into a teacher I had in junior high school. I hadn't seen her in fifteen years, yet she called me by name. Then she asked the dreaded question: "How many children do you have?" "One," I said quietly, quickly adding that my son had been killed. I told her how difficult the Christmas season had been for me, and that I did not expect to ever get over the hurt.

She took my hand and replied, "No, you never will."

I spent a portion of the afternoon immersed in last year's journal. I do not know what possessed me to read segments about my emergency hysterectomy. Perhaps I thought that reading them would shed light on the seemingly permanent encampment of grief in my life. As I read last winter's entries, I wondered if I was being a masochist or a realist.

December 7, 1976

After examining me today, my gynecologist abruptly announced that I needed complete rest for one week. Then she reached for her telephone and booked me into the hospital for an emergency hysterectomy a week from today and a follow-up eight-day hospitalization.

"Why am I supposed to rest if I need an emergency hysterectomy?" I asked.

"I'm afraid you may not survive the operation in your depleted state," she replied with concern.

I caught my breath, not believing what I was hearing. "You mean I m–might d–die?" I stammered.

"Yes," she replied, looking me straight in the eye.

I had no idea the gnawing pain in my side was so serious. I recalled an earlier appointment concerning intense pain I was having after the insertion of an intrauterine device. I was told then that everything was normal. Amid the unbearable pain, I had managed to convince myself that I was being dramatic.

"Rosalie, there's more." The doctor's voice brought me back to the present. "I need to warn you that I strongly suspect you have cancer."

Cancer—such a deadly word, I said to myself. Nobody in my family has *ever* had cancer. "This has to be a mistake," I muttered. "You must have me confused with someone else. I'm only thirty-two years old."

"Rosalie," she said gently. "Listen to me. This is serious. Your life is in jeopardy."

"*Double* jeopardy," I muttered. "I might not survive the operation, and if I do, I might have cancer and die anyway."

"That's the worst that can happen," she said solemnly.

Leaving the office, I felt punished. "I'm too young for all this. What did I do wrong?" I shouted into the empty space of the car. "God, I don't want any part in this drama. All I want is to be normal—to have a normal life and be part of a normal family. Is that too much to ask?" How do I not blame myself? And how do I prepare people for this? were the questions tormenting me as I pulled into the driveway.

Before I had time to formulate a plan, my mother, who had spent most of the afternoon with Kelli-Lynne, opened the back door. "You look ghastly. Did your doctor prescribe medication so you can get some relief from the pain? Do you have another appointment?" My mother's questions tumbled out one after the other.

While attempting to make my way to the door, I looked down at Kelli-Lynne, who was hugging my leg. I felt dizzy and panicky. The possibility that I might never see my daughter grow up invaded my head and body. The sound of Mike's heavy boots on the back porch reminded me that I might not live to see him compete in track this coming spring.

"It's not supposed to be this way. Life is supposed to last," I whispered to myself.

"Rosalie, what's wrong?" my mother interrupted.

I needed to tell someone, because the pounding in my heart felt deafening. But I didn't want to tell my mother all of what the doctor had told me.

Emotionless, I said, "I have to have a hysterectomy."

"When?" she gasped.

"Soon," I muttered. "I have to rest first, because I'm too weak right now." I had intentionally avoided saying, "I'm too weak to survive." I avoided saying anything about cancer, too. At least I had control over *something,* I thought, with gratitude.

"Oh, no, Rosalie," my mother responded. "I was hoping we wouldn't have to go through this again."

"Mom, it's not 'we' who are going through this; it's *me*." I did not want her to be more upset than I was. After all, this was my future, or my death. Certainly, it was my pain.

How will all this be for Kelli-Lynne? I wondered to myself. For Mike, it will be easier, because he is almost fifteen and his life is centered around school, swimming, track, and girls.

"What timing," I groaned. "Convalescing during my favorite season."

I recalled how skillfully I had sent healing to Kelli-Lynne when she was in my womb. Moments after the doctor had announced I was pregnant with her, he advised me to have an abortion, saying, "Rosalie, with all the X rays you've had in the last four weeks, the chances are ninety percent that your child will be born with major deformities, if not chromosomal damage."

Against all odds, I was pregnant. I had no choice but to carry through on my desire to give birth to this baby. Then and there, I decided to quit my teaching job in order to concentrate my energy on the growing life within me.

Today's prognosis sparked another decision: I would spend only three days in the hospital, not nine. For this, I needed support. I called three trusted friends and asked them to surround me with healing energies and to visualize me out of the hospital in three days. At least I'm doing something positive, I reasoned. But silently I wondered if it was too little, too late.

"I'll never be the same," I muttered, shuffling into the kitchen. My mother looked at me strangely. How could I explain that everything around me had taken on an aura of wonder? I was fascinated by the steam rising from the whistling teapot and by my daughter's tiny hands. "I want to remember everything because . . ." I stopped myself from saying the word *death*.

When Gil came home for supper, I was in bed resting, determined to be in good shape for the operation. I bit my lip and told him the doctor suspected cancer. It was the first time I had used the word outside of the doctor's office.

He looked blank. "I'm sure we'll get through this, Rose," he said.

I didn't share his sense of confidence. "What if I don't?" I asked. "We need to talk about what will happen to the children."

"We'll manage," he said casually.

"But I need to talk," I pleaded.

"Get some rest, Rose," he said quietly, closing the bedroom door from the other side.

I was left alone, scared, and angry. I felt like the first kid on the block to need a hysterectomy. Worse yet, everyone I knew who had had cancer was dead. I fell asleep, but woke up intermittently, haunted by images of death and of me running away.

December 8, 1976

I feel ashamed. I hate to complain to friends, so I whine in secret and write in my journal. I torture myself with demands that I should be stronger, or at least more objective. I'm angry and discouraged. I don't know where my voice is. Questions of life and death continue to invade my consciousness, and I resent this crude interruption of my life!

December 14, 1976

I'm drugged. The codeine numbs my body. If I can write, I must be alive, I tell myself.

I remember the beginning of the operation. I was only half anesthetized when the doctor prayed that the knife be guided and we all be protected. I thought she was administering last rites of the church, and tried to remind her that I wasn't Catholic, but my lips were like rubbery licorice, and my words slipped into one another.

When I woke up, my mother said, "It's all over now."

What is? I wondered. I looked down at the bandages covering my abdomen. I was hot, then cold, then hot, like when I was little and had a fever. I wiggled, trying to find a comfortable position. Realizing that I had no feeling in my right leg, I panicked. Oh, God, I thought, what did she take out? What did she leave in? I drifted off to sleep before the answers came.

When I awoke, the doctor was leaning over my bed. "I'm sorry, Rosalie," she said. "There was nothing I could do to save your—" I couldn't remember the rest of the sentence. My *life?* My *ovaries?*

The next time I woke up I discovered, with embarrassment, that I had wet the bed. I was disoriented. I tried to remember what day it was. I tried to remember the details of the operation. I tried to move my right leg, then remembered it wasn't functional. "How is my leg connected to my ovaries?" I mumbled softly.

My mother wiped my forehead. "I'm so hot," I moaned. "And thirsty. Did the doctor come in here, or was I dreaming?"

"She was in to tell you that she had to remove both of your ovaries and your uterus."

I sighed. "But what about the—" I stopped myself, remembering that the cancer was my secret. The word whirled inside me.

"But I'm so hot, and I can't stop being wet," I complained. "And why won't my leg work?" It doesn't make sense, I protested silently. Nobody told me *this* was going to happen!

A nurse appeared, and I asked her for more blankets. "I'm so hot and wet," I told her.

"You're having hot flashes," she calmly explained. "I'll be back with a pill to help you rest more comfortably."

When she returned, I opened my mouth eagerly, then drifted off again until a gentle pressure on my arm connected me to my doctor. She smiled and said, "No cancer, but we've sent specimens for laboratory tests. As far as we can determine, you're clear, but we'll have official results in one week." I sighed. She patted my arm and told me to rest.

The nurse woke me next. She cheerfully asked if I was ready to fill out the birth certificate. I shook my head, unable to articulate the fact that I would never be a new mother again. Apparently I had been placed on the maternity floor of the small hospital. My mother intervened, motioning the nurse toward the door, at which point I fell asleep again.

The next time I opened my eyes, a different nurse was in the room. "When can I go home?" I demanded.

"In a few days," she replied while handing me three more pills.

Gil came in the evening. I tried to stay awake. He looked uncomfortable, so I reassured him that everything was okay. I wanted him to hold my hand, to tell me that the feeling in my leg would return. He talked about the cold weather.

When Gil left, I reached for my journal. My mind was like cement. Do I dare believe that I don't have cancer, or are they waiting for the right time to tell me I do? My insides don't ache so much now, but of course the codeine numbs the pain. As much as I want to project healthy thoughts, I cannot help feeling like a victim. I have been dismembered, and I'll never be able to have another child.

December 15, 1976

The doctor made me look at the scar today. It's ugly, and I was surprised to see how small it is; I expected a big hole. Idly I wondered if I would ever wear a bikini again. The doctor snapped me out of my reverie by delineating the advantages of estrogen pills.

"When would I be able to stop taking them?" I asked.

"In about twenty years," she replied, "but we can reduce the dosage each year."

My greatest hope was to alleviate the assaults of heat that came unexpectedly and left me shivering, so I agreed to the estrogen. This way, I reasoned, the rushes of emotions I was experiencing might dissipate, too.

"Rosie, I want you to forgo sex for five weeks," my doctor said on her way out the door.

What sex? was my first thought. After she left, I felt confused and remorseful. Would I be able to have an orgasm? How would I cope with this sensory loss? I have no clear picture of who I was before the monthly cramps and blood clots began. I know only that I'll never have "my friend" again.

December 17, 1976

I was released from the hospital today because my mother assured the doctor she would look after me. I had escaped in three days—a victory! I called my three healer friends, and we congratulated one another. No matter that I'm constipated and my right leg is still numb . . . I'm out of the hospital, and I'm alive.

December 18, 1976

I have little energy, and I don't know how to explain to Kelli-Lynne that she cannot sit on my lap to cuddle. When she comes close, I hold her hand, smooth her hair, and protect myself from being jostled. Invariably, she bumps into my chair, or pulls my hand too hard or too fast. Then Mai-Tai, our eight-year-old Siamese cat, circles us and tries to jump onto my lap. I'm fine, I tell myself; all this will pass. I'm alive.

December 19, 1976

I feel old. It's as if my memory cells were removed with my ovaries. I've lost continuity with who I was before the operation. This feeling reminds me of the first time I made love with Mike's father. I knew I would never be the same after that. I was changed, rearranged. How odd to associate making love for the first time with the aftermath of a hysterectomy.

December 20, 1976

I'm scared. I never before regarded any part of myself as residing in my female organs. I'm afraid of additional loss. Quickly, I stop feeding these fears. But I don't want to deny them either. I've denied my feelings for too long.

December 22, 1976

I resent having to sit out Christmas. I'm not an invalid, I want to remind people. But then, I am not my usual self yet, either. At this moment, my hair is drenched and perspiration is flooding my chest, face, and back—all because I have refused to take another estrogen pill. I feel like a clown in this wet, red face. I don't even look like myself.

Nothing comforts me. Today a friend joked, "Just think, when we are all wrestling with menopause, you'll be finished." I cannot look ahead fifteen years, especially if I am sentenced to pills for a fifth of a century so as not to drown in my own perspiration.

Why can't I find relief? My organs were rotten, so they were removed. Now, *I* feel rotten and removed. I can't seem to kick the foreboding sense of *what next?* What will I have to lose next? I've turned cynical, and I'm not even preparing for Christmas. Where is my spirit?

December 24, 1976

*M*ike has been a delight. I joined him in the kitchen while he made cookie-dough ornaments for the entire family—crosses with "1976" etched on them. Kelli-Lynne was sleeping, so he and I had some rare private time together. I sense that he is concerned about me but doesn't know how to show it. We are so similar.

I offered to make hot chocolate, but he wanted to make tea for the two of us. I do like receiving from him. I noticed how large his hands have grown and the peach fuzz on his chin and his deep voice.

"Mom, do you think it would be okay to buy Stacie a present, or will she think I'm queer or something?"

I smiled at the image of my fourteen-year-old son presenting a gift to a girl. "I think she would be thrilled if you bought her a present," I told him.

"I still have fifty dollars of my snow-shoveling money, and I can earn more. How much do you think I should spend?"

"What do you plan to buy?" I asked, appreciating that this was an initiation for him.

"I don't know, Mom. What do you think?"

"Mike, I don't know her, but—"

"Yes, you do," he interrupted. "I've introduced you to her at swimming meets, and she came here once after school to listen to records with Artie B. and Scott and me. Remember?"

"Of course I remember, Mike, but I don't know her well enough to think of what she might like."

"Me, neither," he said with a shrug.

"How about a bracelet, or a pin," I suggested.

"Yeah, she likes jewelry. In fact, she said she would order some stuff from me when the track team has its jewelry sale in March. Good idea, Mom. Thanks, Mom."

I was warmed. This is the way it's supposed to be between mother and son. I felt privileged to watch as he worked carefully on each ornament. How long we'd been struggling through the negative, what-do-you-know-anyway stage. But alas, we'd survived.

"Where do I go to buy jewelry and stuff?" he asked.

"Would you like me to go with you?"

"I don't know how to buy anything for a girl. I've never done this before, Mom. Maybe you could help since you're a girl, too. But, Mom, you're not supposed to drive."

I was touched by his concern. "This is special, Mike. We're not going far. Let's see if we can get a babysitter for your sister. We have to hurry. It's already the twenty-fourth of December."

"But what do I do when I give it to her? I'll feel so embarrassed. What if she hasn't bought a present for me, and she feels bad?"

I had forgotten how complicated life is for a teenager. "How about if we find the gift first, *then* figure out how you can give it to her."

"Thanks, Mom. Oh, would you wrap it for me? I'm a slob about wrapping. And I want it to look good."

"Of course," I said as we smiled at each other.

I appreciate the honesty we share in our time together. It seems that when Mike careened into adolescence, I became someone to argue with. I am thankful that our relationship has shifted, and that I am now someone to consult with.

December 27, 1976

Christmas is over, and I accepted my limited participation as well as I could. I was grateful to be released from the cooking, for I still tire easily. Kelli-Lynne received so many gifts that to store them all, we may need to build an addition to the house. Mike is excited about his new ice-fishing gear. He's used the kitchen calendar to mark off the days till his fishing vacation in February.

On Christmas day we had four generations under one roof: my grandparents, my parents, my brother and his wife plus Gil and me, and our children. What a gift it is to come together like this. Now I am certain I will see my children marry and have children, and I will witness my grandchildren having children.

I drifted into sleep thinking about my children's children and grateful to have recovered my optimism. My children are my future, and we are all alive. That is the gift of Christmas 1976!

January 1, 1977

I wonder if my gynecologist removed part of my brain circuitry when she removed my organs. I read today while Kelli-Lynne napped, and although I turned pages, I remembered nothing. The book Bob and I are working on is supposed to be completed by June, but I can't make my mind work.

I torture myself with "shoulds": I should be writing, I should be taking advantage of being home with Kelli-Lynne, I should be preparing for my next workshop, I should be resting. The truth is that I should banish all my shoulds.

January 14, 1977

I want time alone with Gil. But I've been afraid to ask him to escape with me, even for a day, because I expect he'll tell me he's too tired, and I don't want to feel more emotional distance between us than I already do. We've both been tired lately, yet I wonder if some of my fatigue is actually boredom.

When I go out, I share myself with close friends. Yet, I'm saddened and angry that I have to go *out* to do this. I want an intense connection with my husband. Otherwise, what is the meaning of marriage? According to Gil, his marriage is fine; yet his marriage is *my* marriage, and I feel empty.

January 31, 1977

*T*oday I will try a dialoguing technique to give voice to the frustration I have been experiencing in my body.

Me: Whenever I swallow an estrogen pill, I want to throw up. Why did you do this to me, my body? I took care of you pretty well.

My body: Whoever said I came with a lifetime warrantee? You refused to listen to my signals; you denied your pain for years, until it was too late to do anything but operate. Does one breakdown mean you've lost all faith?

Me: I am disillusioned. I took you for granted. I know I am not separate from you, but I don't think of us as a team anymore. I don't even want to be on your team.

My body: Taking me for granted was your problem. I gave you plenty of evidence that you were not as healthy as you pretended. Have you stopped to consider how much better you are feeling since the surgery? You have more energy, less pain, and an appreciation for well-being. So what's the big deal about taking estrogen pills? Or is this struggle more of your need to always be in control?

Me: I resent you, and I hate feeling sentenced to twenty years of swallowing pills from a bottle that carries a cancer warning. Is my only other option to wake up several times each night in a sweat-soaked bed? I'm deprived of sleep and cannot commiserate with anyone. Every woman I know is still in possession of her ovaries and uterus. I feel alone. I am thankful to be alive, but nobody prepared me for *this*.

My body: I admit that I was not on your agenda for the present or the future. You assumed I would be perfect, or at least manageable, until death do us part. Well, I tried my best.

Me: This isn't the way life is supposed to be. You've ruined it! You continue to cause disruption. I want comfort and harmony, and I want to trust you again. This frustration diffuses my energy.

A phone call interrupted my writing. While picking up the receiver I felt clearer, though still unresolved.

February 2, 1977

The consciousness-raising group I have participated in for four years is becoming another source of frustration. The topic today was aging. We talked about reactions to our aging parents and our own feelings of helplessness. Only two of us spoke about our fears: me and a woman who had complications from kidney-stone surgery. We voiced our resentments about our bodies letting us down. I told the group about the anxiety that arises each time I imagine myself embarking on a bodily breakdown. I explained that I hate taking estrogen. "I'm only thirty-two years old, and I have no ovaries and no uterus," I said earnestly. The intensity of my feelings scared me.

Someone hushed me with the message that I should be thankful I don't have cancer. Someone else comforted me by saying I don't have to use contraceptives anymore. I nodded my head passively, though I felt like screaming, How dare my body interrupt my life! I can appreciate that some old people become cantankerous. As long as they're angry and insist on being heard, they know they are alive. Resistance is more life affirming than resignation.

I want to be real. I want to express my outrage and feel free to be irrational. I want cheerleaders beside me while I throw a tantrum. Without support for my outrage, I will only accommodate the desires of others. What I need most is support and permission to grieve the loss of my organs. What I receive is platitudes.

February 16, 1977

I've been reading *Hero with a Thousand Faces* by Joseph Campbell. As a result, I'm coming to regard my hysterectomy as a heroine's voyage into the unknown. The journey I am undergoing seems composed of four distinct stages. First, *concern:* Did I have cancer? Second, *relief:* No cancer, but no organs either. Third, *resentment:* Why me? Why hormones? And fourth, *reinvestment:* Reengaging in life through writing and exercise.

By picturing my hysterectomy as a journey, I hope to become more patient with myself and more sensitive. I do believe in initiations and rituals, but I wonder, What am I being initiated *into?*

March 3, 1977

*M*ike planned and hosted my thirty-third birthday party. During his February vacation, he went ice fishing, hooked ten fish, and secreted them away in a friend's freezer. Then he invited family members and friends to a surprise birthday feast at our house.

When the day arrived, he was so excited that he even kissed me on the cheek after I blew out the candles on the cake he had made.

"This is the way it's supposed to be," I whispered to both of us.

He looked embarrassed when I opened his gift. "I hope you like it," he said. "It reminded me of Indians and power, and I thought you liked turquoise. It's not queer to buy a ring for your mother, is it, Mom?"

I smiled, hugged him, and said, "I love it, Mike. I'm glad you gave it to me."

"Just in case you didn't like it, I found these plant pots for the kitchen window. See? They hang and everything." He tripped over his big feet as he handed them to me, and my brother snapped a picture. Mike then announced that he had bought a new roll of film so that we would have plenty of pictures. He had thought of everything.

Before the day ended, I told Mike how happy I was. Maybe now that I am a new thirty-three and he is almost a new fifteen, we can show our love and respect for each other. I think we are both tired of quarreling.

The year that bridged the loss of my ability to birth a child with the death of my son is now officially over. The period of questioning life and death, however, is not.

January 1, 1978

Loneliness, truth, and the creative process are interwoven. When I do not speak my truth, I compromise myself. Then I get angry, cut off my anger, and isolate myself. Most often, I set myself up with my family. When I begin to tell them who I am and what I am feeling, they argue. At times I give in to being who they think I am. Why don't I simply tell them, "I feel empty and alone when I am with you, and I want to feel connected"?

January 3, 1978

More dreams. In the first, I was baking bread. I substituted spaghetti squash for flour. The finished loaf was unique and delicious. Everyone who tried it was impressed. "How did you do it?" they wanted to know. "Where did you get the idea?" "May I have the recipe?"

I casually replied, "I used what was available. All the ingredients were simply around."

In the second dream, I was attending a conference in Florida. The person at the podium asked, "Who can teach Parent Effectiveness Training?" I raised my hand. She then asked, "Who can teach Affective Education Training?" Again I raised my hand. "Who has the credentials to teach a course on journal-keeping?" I raised my hand once more.

The woman looked at me and said, "Then you must be Dr. Fish." Before I could reply, she remarked, "But you don't look like *Dr. Fish*. You look too normal and too young." She invited me to take over, and without preparation, I began. I spoke from experience. I was my only reference point.

What do I make of these two dreams? To begin with, my sun sign is Pisces, two fish. Because of my Piscean nature, I am endowed with intuition and compassion. I already have all the ingredients needed to teach, to reach, to be. Using my dreams as a springboard for action, I hereby resolve to create a situation in which I can teach by drawing on what I know.

January 5, 1978

This morning I met with the dean of the college I teach at, and proposed a new elective: Journal-Keeping as Creative Problem Solving. She
agreed to run a description of the course in the upcoming curriculum
guide. I look forward to working with others in this way, and being paid
for it!

My adopted spiritual mother, Liz, surprised me with a visit this afternoon. I enjoyed our time together, though I worry about her. She spoke
about her fears of dying before having "done enough mothering."
Instinctively I know she is preparing for her own death. I am sad and
powerless, yet I'm glad Liz confided in me. This new feature in our relationship is welcome—I am family to her, and families should be places
of realness.

January 7, 1978

Kelli-Lynne cried when I left her at the library for story hour. As I
drove off, my ears buzzed with the phrase "Fear is not having enough
of your mother." Now I wonder, Do we, as children, ever have enough?
I'm a full-time mom until my daughter starts school, but I do need some
time to myself.

Ever since Mike died, I have focused most of my time and energy
on Kelli-Lynne. I have allowed her to fill up the holes in my life, and
have stopped whatever I'm doing to be with her. To a large extent I've
been using her, and she's acted her role perfectly. We need to learn
how to be both together and separate.

January 8, 1978

Do I retreat into dreams because my daily life is so stale, or do my
dreams preview an emerging reality? Actually, I want to believe in
myself, and since my dreams reflect my brightness, I thrive on them!

In last night's dream, I was wearing a long, tight blue dress and
dancing with a man I did not recognize. We moved in perfect rhythm
without speaking. He swung me high in the air. Surprised, excited, and
embarrassed, I wondered if my underpants were showing.

Our dance was an art form; together we were a unity. Suddenly, however, I was on the other side of the ballroom floor realizing the need to create movements distinct from my partner's. I glided into the winged motions of a huge bird. I swirled solo in circles. Then I rejoined my partner.

What dance am I being invited to participate in? I asked myself when I awoke at 2:13 in the morning. Sleepily, I asked for a clarifying dream, giving thanks in advance. The answer came in the shape of a huge fire-breathing dragon. I was fascinated as I studied this creature with shimmering skin. "You need me, and I need you" was its message.

In the dream this statement made sense. But now I cannot fathom why I would need a dragon or a dragon would need me. I associate dragons with magic, power, creatures to be slain before a maiden is saved. Who, or what, are my dragons? Do I have to slay one, or do I have to slay parts of myself? The truth is that I already feel slain.

January 24, 1978

I search to understand how I sabotage myself. I have been sick with strep throat and bronchitis. My mother offered to help, so I allowed her to nurture me for nine days. She fluffed my pillow, concocted eggnogs, administered medicine, and entertained Kelli-Lynne while I slept . . . and slept. Only a few times did I awaken to compile mental lists of what needed to be done. Mostly I was missing Mike.

At one point Kelli-Lynne came up to me and said, "Mom, the only thing we can do is love Mike lots and miss him a little." I have no idea how she knew what was going on. When she later tiptoed back into my room, she squeezed my hand and begged me not to die, too. I promised her once again that I would not leave her. Something about that promise elicited the will to be well. Kelli-Lynne is certainly pulling me through!

I'm too tired to confront the death throes of my marriage. Losing Mike was sudden and unexpected; my marriage feels like a terminal illness. I want the chance to love, not leave. I want the chance to live, not lose. I want to dance, but my partner is not interested in dancing.

I search through books, scouting for a direction. At the same time, I know that only I can dictate my course. I imagine approaching people on the street, saying, "Pardon me, I seem to have misplaced my spirit. Have you seen her?" (In folklore dragons are often female.) Is the dragon of my dream a metaphor for my spirit? Can one dance with one's spirit?

January 31, 1978

I've arranged for Kelli-Lynne to attend a co-operative nursery school three mornings a week, starting in March. My challenge will be to avoid giving my time away to others. Let there be balance!

Last week everything I tried to do was obstructed. The tub ran over as I was washing clothes in the laundry. I started to bake cookies, then discovered I was out of eggs. My head feels stuffed with cotton, and I am detached from people. I also have more intense chest pains. I made an appointment to see my doctor because I'm afraid of a heart attack. In one sense, it's interesting that my heart chakra is under attack. My heart, the most direct link to my spirit, is cut off. No wonder I have a hard time getting out of my own way!

Today I took action. I washed floors, mopped, vacuumed, and dust-ed. But as always, something occurs at the expense of something else—although the house is no longer encrusted with crud, I have spent no time writing and precious little time with Kelli-Lynne. I need a wife.

February 1, 1978

My doctor confirmed that my heart is sound and my vital signs are good. I told her about Mike's death, and she suggested that I take tran-quilizers until I feel "more in control." I refused. A daily dose of estrogen is insult enough. Am I being rigid about the wrong things? I think I will compromise by taking stress-reducing B vitamins.

February 6, 1978

My energy is increasing. Maybe it's because of the vitamins, or perhaps because I know I will have more time to myself when Kelli-Lynne starts nursery school next month.

Today I moved Mike's desk into the spare room adjoining Kelli-Lynne's bedroom. I tacked along the walls large strips of white paper, which Kelli-Lynne proceeded to decorate with her crayons. I write as she chatters to me and colors in her designs. Fragmentation is built into my days. I look around at other mothers at home with their children; our lives are as predictable as chicken soup. Having spent years juggling my time and scattering my energy, I am determined to bring more focus and action to my days.

Currently, my greatest interruption is the telephone. When Kelli-Lynne was an infant, I took the phone off the hook while nursing her. These days the phone remains operative round the clock, even when she is at play group and I have a potential block of time to myself. Now I would not dare to disengage the phone. What if she died, and I sat here unreachable?

February 7, 1978

The struggle continues to create a time of quietness in which to attend to my internal rhythms. I need the opportunity to listen, to cry, to question without judgment. I want to practice gentleness and acceptance.

I am interested in attending a weekend workshop called Body-Centered Psychotherapy. Training sessions of this sort were easy to justify when I was employed full-time and earning money. Now that I am working part-time, I'm not sure I deserve to invest money in my education.

When I told Gil I wanted to talk this evening, he looked worried, but agreed. I explained that since I'm not working full-time, I feel guilty about spending money on workshops, and at the very least I want to be free to write a few nights a week, which means that he would have to take responsibility for Kelli-Lynne and the dishes. Requesting time off for writing seemed extremely indulgent.

February 8, 1978

I toy with the idea of designing a week-long workshop entitled Women and Creativity. It would tie together two themes: how women are socialized to avoid expressing "negative" emotions, such as anger and jealousy, and how unprepared we are to leave relationships. Anger, it seems, is always present in transitions, as is sadness. Until these emotions are acknowledged and expressed, all transitions remain incomplete. The workshop would highlight creative ways of articulating anger and sadness.

As I look back on my own life, I can see the posture I dutifully maintained after Mike's death. I did not express my outrage at the power company, at Mike, at God, at Artie B. for not intervening, or at my family for being so rigid. Instead, I turned the anger inward and began feeling guilty and depressed. My lines read: "If I only had been a better mother, Mike would have survived. Therefore, I will be a dedicated mom to Kelli-Lynne. If I am not a perfect mother, she might die and I will be punished again by death." Only now am I beginning to see that I do not have the power to guarantee the life of my children.

Allowing Gil to take over at night so I can have time to myself feels like a step in the right direction. The icicles are melting, and some of the tightness in my heart is dissipating.

February 11, 1978

I try not to overreact to Kelli-Lynne's barrage of death questions. She asks if I know when I am going to die, if I know when she is going to die, if she will die before I do, if I think Mike wants us all to die. I imagine she knows something I don't, and these questions are her way of preparing me for that eventuality.

February 12, 1978

*N*ot only did I attend the Body-Centered Psychotherapy workshop but it became a meeting place for the person I thought I was and the person I really am. The confrontation unfolded gradually. We began with relaxation techniques. Once relaxed, we were encouraged to say to ourselves, "I am," and to feel a positive part of ourselves. Instantly I said, "I am creative." My body responded with a surge of energy, my face felt hot, and my heart rushed. I had the urge to move forward. When Ron Kurtz, the leader, gently asked us to identify the opposing feeling, I said, "I am rigid." My whole body constricted—my pelvis tightened, my shoulders and knees locked in place, and my breathing became labored. Experiencing my own rigidity, I felt small and too embarrassed to say how minuscule I felt; refusing to tell, however, kept me rigid. Ron then instructed us to move from the positive posture ("I am creative") to the negative ("I am rigid"), and to notice the point at which the balance shifted. My shifting point was shrouded in a foglike mist. I tried to envision other images, but the fogginess remained. Now I'm puzzled. Why mist?

Inherent in mist is hope.

After taking note of the shifting point, I saw an image of a butterfly with folded wings. Its position reminded me of the womblike knee-to-chest, head-down posture I often assume when scared, hoping nobody will see inside me. When I examined the butterfly more closely, an eagle emerged—free, powerful, and majestic in its flight. Suddenly I became the eagle, and propelled by instinct and mastery, I soared toward the light. Along the way, I encountered the shimmering dragon of my dreams. I giggled, because we were dancing in harmony. I had the impulse to sing the song "Me and My Shadow" when I realized with stunning clarity that my power and grace were indeed my shadows!

After lunch, Ron outlined his theory of letting go. Love's energy is tapped only after grief has been expressed, he said. Once love is realized and articulated, energy for sex becomes available, and joy and reverence follow naturally.

Ron then led us through walking exercises designed to help us become aware of where we "hold" emotions in the body. I discovered that I hold love, grief, and anger in my chest, right next to my heart. I couldn't distinguish between these emotions. To get to the core of my rigidity, I realized, I would have to begin with anger.

Ron asked for volunteers to demonstrate an anger exercise, and before I could think, I stood up. Pillows were piled around me, and three people offered to be my "guards" so I wouldn't hurt myself. I began to pound the pillows with my fists, then with my feet. My jaw was clenched tight, and my eyes squeezed shut so I wouldn't see what I was doing. Immediately an image of my father appeared. I screamed at him, "Damn you!" Someone whispered, "Yell *louder*" while pressing on my belly. I screamed the words again, pounding the pillows with renewed strength. My voice seemed to be coming from my toes. Then an image of Mike appeared, and I yelled, "Damn you for dying. Damn you, damn you!" at which point tears flooded my body.

Someone prompted me to stay with anger a little longer, and what rushed in this time was a picture of *me*. I became vehemently angry at myself for being angry! I thrashed around on the pillows, kicking and yelling. Then I was engulfed by a picture of Mike in his coffin, and I started to weep. I cried with my mouth open wide and my eyes tightly closed. One person cradled my head while another wiped away my tears. I was too limp to resist, too exhausted to say thank you.

I struggled against opening my eyes. What would everyone think of me for carrying on in this way? I trembled, because I had broken a family rule: never make a scene. Squeezing my eyes shut even more tightly, I heard, "You're okay, Rosie." Reluctantly, I raised my eyelids. My three helpers were looking at me through moist eyes. They hadn't collapsed or run away! Even though I was angry and devastated, everyone had stayed with me.

Perhaps this means that I can grieve and people will remain by my side. Clearly, I don't have to minimize my feelings to take care of anyone, including myself.

February 16, 1978

The past several days have been jam-packed with tight schedules, so today, when Kelli-Lynne announced that she wanted to wear pajamas "all day long" and "never go anywhere," I delighted us both by saying, "As long as I don't have to get dressed, either." We giggled like two little kids sharing an important secret. And we spent the day in our pj's.

This evening I saw a client, and marveled at my skills as a counselor. As long as I stay aligned with my intuition, I am focused and smooth, and I can serve as a guide.

February 19, 1978

I went to see the movie *Equus* and found the plot riveting, perhaps because the lead character was Mike's age. I watched closely to see what part the mother played in her son's crime, all the while wondering about my own role in the plot of Mike's death.

When will the questions end? When will death simply *be?*

When you disenfranchise yourself from having a part in it.

I breathed deeply. I was not present when Mike died. For the first time in nearly a year, I do not feel guilty about being unable to ensure my son's life.

February 22, 1978

Gil and I looked at modular homes today. I should have predicted he would say they were all too expensive. Whether the price is right or not, I am determined to move away from this house. I don't need to sit on the deck and look out on the school yard, or glance out the kitchen window to the spot where my son died.

The day wasn't a total disappointment. We visited a couple whose son was electrocuted a few years ago. They had called us shortly after Mike's death, offering comfort and inviting us to visit them whenever we were ready. With them, I felt safe. I wasn't tempted to keep them from feeling my pain—or their own.

March 1, 1978

*O*ur chance for a new beginning has materialized! We placed a bid on a new house, contingent on the sale of our present house. Today I methodically began painting the woodwork, cleaning the ceiling, and tending to a host of other cosmetic repairs I'd been ignoring all these years. This house has never looked so good! I know that the first people who walk in the door will buy it. In addition to being excited, I feel queasy planning a move without Mike.

March 16, 1978

*A*s I suspected, the first couple to walk through the house bought it. So today I made a ritual of saying good-bye to the house that has been my home for five years, the house that witnessed Kelli-Lynne's birth and Mike's death. I walked through each room carrying a white candle and a handful of salt. I recited memories as they came alive, and I scattered salt to neutralize the energy. I don't know where this ritual came from; perhaps I have always known it.

Why does the movement of my life resemble a funeral dirge? Carl Jung claimed that we do not come to consciousness without pain. Others write that crisis precedes transformation. I do believe that every act has a purpose, that a crisis can lead to knowledge. My own process of growth demands that I leave behind what I no longer need. But how do I do this creatively? Neatly? I need to forge a geography of my consciousness so I can differentiate between selfishness and self-direction.

One year ago today my son died. I know how to celebrate birthdays, but I have no guidelines for honoring death days. Gil agreed to take the morning off so we could be together.

We dropped Kelli-Lynne off at a neighbor's house and went out for breakfast. At first everything felt awkward. I admitted that I didn't know how to do whatever it was we were doing. I wanted us to talk about Mike, to remember him together. Gil wanted to talk about the weather. I wanted to discuss how we as a family are surviving. Gil wanted to know what was in the muffins he was eating. I wanted to address our pain; he complained about the cost of the food.

Turning away to hide my tears of disappointment, I spotted a photograph on the far wall. The image reminded me of Mike and the significance of this occasion. Without a word, I slipped off for a closer look. It was a picture of the sun setting over a watery marsh, clouds of apricot-gray shading the landscape, and a ray of apricot-orange light blazing a beacon across still, gray water. The meaning was simple: sunset marks the end of day, and a ray of sunlight brings the promise of morning.

Noting that the photograph was for sale, I motioned for Gil to come take a look at it. I hoped he would appreciate the symbolism as much as I did. Instead he remarked, "Who would ever pay thirty dollars for a photograph?"

"I would," I said. Quickly I wrote a check and handed it to the cashier before Gil could convince me that I was being foolishly sentimental. As we left the restaurant, picture in hand, Gil looked at his watch and said, "If you don't need me anymore, I have a lot to do at work."

"But it's only ten o'clock," I replied.

"Rose, we can't sanctify this day because Mike happened to have died on the twenty-third of March last year."

"Gil, I'm not asking that we sanctify it, but I want to spend time talking with you and being together."

"We did, and now breakfast is over," he said sharply.

"I'm on my own then," I said.

He nodded.

I dropped him off at work, bundled up, and drove to Two Lights. On impulse, I stopped at a flower shop and bought one long-stemmed red rose to toss into the frigid ocean.

After casting the rose into the waves, I wrote the following poem:

> *Without you, never would I have experienced*
>   *the emotional roller coaster of mothering a son.*
> *Without you, never would I have committed myself*
>   *to living and loving fully.*
> *Without you, never would I have tasted*
>   *the poignancy of grief.*
> *Without you, never would I have entered*
>   *the abyss of loneliness.*
> *Without you, I would only have half lived my life.*

As soon as I had penned the last line, a shorter poem appeared at the bottom of the page:

> Oncoming waves rush to fill the abyss,
> Like me, swirling to fill the crevassed edges of grief.

During the afternoon, I stayed by the telephone, hoping to hear words of comfort from my mother or grandmother. The telephone did not ring. Gil came home for supper, then announced that he was going out drinking with my brother to commemorate the day.

"But what about me?" I asked sullenly.

"You don't like beer, Rose."

"That's not what I mean, Gil. I don't want to stay home alone, especially tonight," I pleaded.

"You're not alone. Kelli-Lynne is here."

I was angry, and couldn't believe what I was hearing. Grief is lived separately. When will I learn that I am on my own?

As soon as Gil left, my best friend called. She had remembered the day. After speaking with her, I put Kelli-Lynne to bed and poured myself a glass of wine. If Gil can get drunk, I can, too, I thought, but decided that drinking wasn't my way of honoring Mike. Instead, I lit two white candles, perfumed the air with sandalwood incense, sat on a cushion, and listened to Mahler's Ninth Symphony (*Resurrection Symphony*). As the first refrain sounded, I picked up my pen and wrote:

Twisting, pulsating, riveting,
Isolating, persevering, descending
Into the entrails of my beginnings.
Swallowing, suffocating, vomiting
Into my own darkness.
Wobbling, persevering,
To reawaken Illumination.
Amidst the echoes of Advice-givers, I retreat
To respond instead to a faint, familiar sound:
A note housed within my body-memory that
Resounds through the echoes of Darkness.
My journey back to my beginnings
Promises to take me to my depths.
Clothed within a nuance of hesitation,
I once more silently commit to seek
The meaning of the elusive note
Which echoes within
Like a shadow cast on a hazy day.
No Exits.
The promise is merged with the pain.
And pain merges with promise.

I honored the anniversary of Mike's death with poetry and tears. My mother never called. Gil hasn't come home. And in eighteen minutes, the day that Mike died one year ago will be over.

Conflict has been a taboo area for women. Women are supposed to be the quintessential accommodators, mediators, the adapters and soothers. Yet conflict is necessary if women are to build for the future.
—Jean Baker Miller

Year Two

April 19, 1978

I want to believe that our family of three can survive. The purpose of buying a different house is to build a future in a new neighborhood with a view of the ocean to replace that of the school yard. I am concerned about my marriage, but perhaps that, too, needs a change of scene.

May 4, 1978

Last year on Mike's birthday, we scattered his ashes. This year, we moved into a house on the corner of Channel and Cloister roads, less than a mile from our old neighborhood. I promised our former neighbors I would visit, but I knew I wouldn't. My desire was to be free of memories.

After seven hours of loading and unloading boxes, I realize there is no escape from memories. I couldn't leave behind Mike's baseball glove, or his minnow traps, or his bicycle.

∞ ∞

June 5, 1978

All our energy and money are being siphoned into bringing this house back to life. I tire myself out working on the exterior renovation, and all the while I pretend that my interior is undergoing renovation as well. If I had courage, I would say, "I've made another mistake."

June 19, 1978

I've returned to teach at the Creative Problem Solving Institute. I will be instructing people who in the past taught me, and I want to be relaxed, because I know that enjoyment enhances effectiveness. With that in mind I redesigned my two-and-a-half-hour session many times.

Last night I dreamed that I was teaching a large group of people. I was well prepared and confident. I placed my lesson plan on the overhead projector, then ripped it up, saying, "This programmed approach is what creativity *isn't*." I encouraged the class to listen to tapes of music I had brought and furnished art materials to use in portraying their experiences. Finally I invited them to dance their insights. I woke up feeling exhilarated. Will I have the courage, I wondered, to carry out my dream message?

I was afraid no one would attend my session because ten others were being offered at the same time. When I walked in, however, the room was crowded. I had dressed carefully in a white blouse and white slacks. As I was greeted by my former teachers, I told myself, They're here to support you, not to judge you. The papers I clutched in my shaking hand made a fanning sound. I took a deep breath, shared with the group last night's dream, and ripped up my lesson plan for the day. We had begun!

Without notes, I had more energy to devote to the group. Instinctively, I knew the natural moments for silence, the time for music and movement. I participated in the movement sequence, feeling deeply connected to the spirit of Mike and to my own creative process. In some inexplicable way, I thought Mike was providing inspiration for the session.

July 6, 1978

$\mathscr{I}$ don't know what to make of last night's dream, yet I can't dismiss it from my thoughts. I was at the beach, watching huge waves crash against the shore. Fascinated by the power and rhythm of the waves, I realized suddenly that I could choose to look either at them or at the spaces between the trillions of water molecules that formed them.

Glancing over my left shoulder, I was terrified to discover a giant mountain of sand accumulating on the beach directly behind me. I panicked, knowing I would suffocate as it moved toward me. Looking frantically at the ocean, I saw enormous tidal waves. Death by either suffocation or drowning was inevitable. I felt both doomed by and in awe of the magnification of natural forces. Then a rainbow created a bridge between the sand and ocean, and by stepping onto this bridge I was able to find safety.

I am ready to admit that I have no control over life and death. Raised to believe that I must be in charge of my emotions and my environment, I am now convinced that all my beliefs are being tested. I am willing to admit that a force greater than me has taken over and is directing the course of events in my world.

July 10, 1978

$\mathscr{R}$ecognizing dreams as my most profound teachers, I asked for one that would help me find direction in life. In the answer dream, I was driving a car. To arrive at my destination, I had to pass through a tunnel. Entering the tunnel, I became afraid, impatient, and excited about what was on the other side. Then I realized that the car's headlights were not working. I drove along very carefully. Three-quarters of the way through, I saw a narrow opening in the wall and a sign for Mystic Tunnel. At that moment, white and yellow lights penetrated my body. I felt transparent, and sensed that this was the energetic meaning of the word *godhead*.

After that, I was taken to a temple of healing, where I heard the words: "Always before, when you have worked with healing, you've done it for others. Now you are purifying yourself with our assistance. Be at peace with yourself, and you will resonate with healing energies."

The word *healing* sounds arrogant to me. What do I know about mystics? The "godhead energy" feels more in keeping with my experience. It reminds me of my fascination with the transcendental poets of the nineteenth century.

July 12, 1978

My grandparents and parents attempt to rewrite history; I try to stay honest and sane. My grandparents have ordered a large bronze plaque imprinted with Mike's name, birth date, and death date. They plan to place it in the family burial plot "so that Mike will have a resting place and the family can visit him," my grandmother told me.

"He has been cremated, and his ashes have been scattered at Two Lights State Park. He is not buried where you'll be planting the marker, Nanny," I said with a depth of emotion that surprised me.

"To us he is," my grandmother replied. "The marker will be ready by September, when we plan to have a family ceremony."

"Nanny, I won't be there. I can't pretend. And I don't want Kelli-Lynne to grow up believing her brother is buried somewhere he isn't."

Then my mother announced plans to put an engraved plaque for Mike in his favorite tree at their camp and to post a sign naming the area "Mike's Cove."

It seems unhealthy to pour so much time and energy into honoring someone who is dead. My parents' and grandparents' houses are crowded with pictures of Mike. Don't the living matter, too? I want to tell them that they cannot enshrine Mike. I want to tell them that I need their cooperation. Without it, I am apt to get caught up in make-believe.

No two people grieve alike. I cannot support my family in the way they work out their sadness; nor do they support me. I thought tragedy brought people closer together.

August 3, 1978

*Y*esterday someone asked me what my heart's desire is. "To be loved and loving," I replied without thinking.

September 1, 1978

*D*arkness descends early, neighbors wed themselves to chain saws, and neat stacks of wood appear overnight. The large maple tree at the top of the street boasts bright orange leaves. Autumn is here, and another school year is about to begin. Although we are in a different neighborhood, I have not been spared the pain of missing Mike. When I think of him entering the eleventh grade, my heart feels as broken as it did last year.

A friend once told me that each journey begins with a question. If only I could ask the *right* question, I might be able to move. One of the principles underlying the *I Ching*, the Chinese Book of Changes, is that we live through an infinity of experiences with the same meaning until we've learned a particular lesson. Is my lesson about losing or leaving or loving? Are they one and the same?

September 12, 1978

A ritual is needed for divorce. I accompanied a friend to the judge's chambers today. Questions were asked, a gavel pounded, and in three minutes a fourteen-year marriage was over. So much for the physical components of a relationship, but what about the emotional ones?

For me, growth takes place outside of marriage, and within it I'm lonely. Even when Gil and I work on the house, we station ourselves in separate rooms, if not different floors. When we're together, I sometimes wonder if I'm becoming celibate. I'm neither excited nor excitable. Making love is simply not worth the effort it requires. Do all marriages end after the sudden death of a child, or is sexual excitement just one more thing I'm losing?

September 15, 1978

*W*hile driving home from exercise class today, I somehow ended up behind a hearse. My knuckles turned white as I clutched the steering wheel. I wondered why I had refused to ride in the hearse when Mike's body was transported from the hospital to the funeral home, and why I chose to avoid following it from the funeral home to the crematorium— both regrettable decisions on my part.

A red light halted the flow of traffic. To stop myself from looking at the hearse, I concentrated on a group of teenagers who had gathered at the curb. A boy I didn't recognize waved, putting his finger to his lips as if to hush the others. Were they Mike's friends? I wondered. Were they remembering, too? When the light turned green, I pulled to the side of the road. My eyes were filled with tears. I felt the pain all over again. This time I decided to allow the tears to flow.

September 20, 1978

Gil's vacation starts in a few days, and we've made no plans thus far. He is consumed with home repairs. "We need renovation too, Gil," I say. He shrugs and walks out of the room. I suggest a few days at my parents' camp; he refuses. Clearly, he does not want to be alone with me.

September 28, 1978

I feel like crying, and I don't want to cry alone. Gil avoids me. He told me today that he's afraid I will ask him to comfort me, and he feels helpless.

"You don't have to *say* anything," I offered. "You don't have to *do* anything. Just hold me." He shrugged and disappeared into the yard. I'm destined to cry alone.

October 1, 1978

I'm purging. My desk has been covered with letters to answer, proposals to submit, course outlines, plans for new books. Today I answered letters, completed a couple of strategies for classroom teachers, filed some ideas for future development, and tossed away papers I knew I would never use. I feel satisfied in mind and heart!

October 3, 1978

Accompanied by Chris Williamson's song "The Changer and the Changed" and unencumbered by clothes, I painted my bedroom a gentle blue. The lyrics "The tender lady has sadness in her eyes" reminded me of my depths and "Please give her happiness and peace of mind" seemed the call of my heart. This is *my bedroom,* I announced to myself, pleased with the outcome. I giggled when I saw my body covered with blue spots.

October 15, 1978

I was about to begin teaching an assertiveness training course I had designed, and I was shaking from head to toe. I told my first class that I was nervous. I also explained that you must know what you are feeling before you can know what you need. "Asking for what you need," I emphasized, "is the last step in the process." I loved using my experience to point out principles. Two and a half hours whizzed by.

October 18, 1978

*S*hortly after Kelli-Lynne was born, I promised myself I'd return to my junior high school teaching position. I didn't. Nor would I now, for I have little interest in perpetuating the myth of the strong lady. No way could I convey the message, "See how well I cope? I can nurture teenagers who happen to be the age of my dead son."

Preparation was the theme of last night's dream. I was teaching a course in psychic development and demonstrating ways to center diffused energy. Simultaneously I was being prepared by those in the spirit realm. I woke up feeling excited.

November 14, 1978

"*I*mpulsive"—that's the word used by two women in the consciousness-raising group upon learning of my decision to participate in a workshop entitled Music, Meditation, and Acid. In self-defense I tried to explain why I, who have never smoked marijuana, would voluntarily take LSD. "I need to do my grieving," I said earnestly. "I can talk circles around my pain, and I'm too controlling. I need to break through. Besides, Walter—the man who conducts the workshop—uses acid as a tool to help participants experience their own mystical qualities."

The women voiced their fears. I responded by explaining that probably anything would be better than the waking numbness I feel. I told them about the autobiography I'd have to write, the pictures of myself

I'd have to bring, even the twenty-four-hour introductory fast. Nothing swayed them.

"Naturally, I'm scared," I said in a shaky voice, "but this is a super-vised workshop, and the acid has been clinically tested. I have to do this. I trust myself, my timing, and my purpose." I concluded by pointing out that I believe purity of intention is a form of protection, but they remained fearful.

Here I am in a consciousness-raising group, unable to elicit support! I am beginning to see that though safety may be sought in the familiar—in the fold of family, marriage, and friends—it is not always *found* there.

November 26, 1978

The workshop opened with a meditation. Following that, we were instructed to partake of our "sacrament" of acid. I toyed with the idea of not swallowing the small white tablet, but decided to push beyond resis-tance. Looking down, I noticed a tiny black spider dashing across the face of my watch. A sign of transformation, I concluded.

As I snuggled into my sleeping bag, my eyes covered with a blind-fold, I was tense. I wanted to surrender to the music that was playing, but the note-taker in me strove to mentally record all proceedings. Eventually my body seemed to melt and the tension disappeared, so much so that I had to rub my hands together to assure myself that I could still feel.

The music vibrated through my body, producing colors with each note. A cloud of swirling, lush aqua blue and chocolate brown sur-rounded me. I became absorbed in the colors. Then my attention was drawn to a sandpainting. Very soon, however, the design shifted, and as it did, my body resonated with the changes. I merged with the sand-painting, as if I were being poured through an hourglass. In syncopat-ed rhythm, a medley of brilliantly colored mandalas, like stained-glass embroidery, encircled me, inviting me to dance. As I relaxed, the man-dalas transformed into many sandpaintings. The designs on top were perfect, yet beneath each one was another sandpainting that added even more beauty and dimension.

I listened to a song about a girl running away from home. I experi-enced myself as the runaway daughter, then as the mother, then as the mother of the mother, and finally as the daughter of the daughter.

Everyone fused, and my heritage stretched into eternity. To the extent that anything happens to one, I realized, it happens to all.

As if on some cosmic cue, Mike entered as a ray of white light. I recognized him as my son, and we bowed to each other in a timeless gesture of honoring. We glided into play like two children, flying effortlessly, then swimming. A deep and eternal bond linked us. Tears flowed along my light-ray body. "We both did the best we could with who we were," Mike said. "How could you expect to give me a part of yourself that you never knew?"

He understood more about me than I did. "I wish we had been able to relate like this when we were together," I lamented.

"It was the only way it could have been," he relayed with wordless energy, and the truth of his statement vibrated throughout my body.

Mike waved his "hand," and created a mandala exactly like the ones I had admired earlier. I waved my "hand," and created a rainbow. We applauded each other, and continued to swap magic in a free and playful way. I knew we were allies. I also knew we were destined to learn from each other.

Again we soared, this time taking our places in a pattern of mandalas that extended to infinity. The mandalas formed a chain, and Mike and I were the links that clipped the chain together. Instead of working on my grief as I had planned, I was infused with the spirit of unity and love, aglow with the joy inherent in evolution.

As the music entered me a second time, I left Mike easily. The notes triggered colors that penetrated different parts of my body. I saw myself as an infant being rocked in a cradle slung between two trees; blinding white light surrounded me. I was high on a mountaintop, with people who loved and appreciated my essence. My caretakers understood my affinity with the universe. I was home at last!

Unexpectedly, my biological parents appeared, and I stiffened. In response, my spiritual caretakers demonstrated with cobwebs how I existed within the pattern of the universe. My biological parents saw and understood this association, and I forgave them for not feeling the sense of cosmic union that was my birthright.

Then suddenly I was a thirty-four-year-old woman. Music shot through my body. I danced effortlessly, embodying pure movement, sexuality, and grace. Intense feelings of my own sacredness and sensuousness merged.

"Now. At last. You see," someone pronounced.

I was at the center of an intricate cobweb, sending out fibers of my being that emitted a green mist. This mist, I understood, was a powerful healing essence. Instantly I became a solitary lighthouse. I watched myself change from being the lighthouse to being the light. As the beacon shined on distant lands, they transformed. The power of the light enlivened me.

Without warning, I became a patient on a psychiatric ward. From all around me I could hear whispered conversations about my inability to return from the acid trip. One psychiatrist said that my investigations into creativity were ironic, because I would never be creative again. I intuited that my friends were close by, anxiously awaiting my return. I tried to converse with them, but my words were muffled, producing a babble they regarded as further evidence of my craziness.

I was aware of being held up by a tight circle of allies who were baptizing me with sunlight. Their arms stretched into space. Looking again, I noticed that their arms had become lilies and lotus blossoms. Beautiful circles of white light surrounded me. I knew I was expected to look at this powerful light, to let it sink into the backs of my eyes so it could be reflected outward through my pupils as healing energy. Squinting to avoid burning my eyes, I watched. At first I became the lighthouse beacon again. Then green mist gushed gently from my body while a voice echoed, "She's finally seeing herself as a healer."

Absorbed by ebbing and flowing movements. I wove in and out with no memory of where I was or where I had been. I danced and swayed with the awkwardness of a seven year old. Then I was thirty-seven, dancing with sweeping grace and wisdom. Then I was seventy-seven—small, wrinkled, and exuding beauty as I moved to and fro. I watched the three Rosies dance instinctively to the music, in perfect time. Every atom of my being imploded with reverence.

Mike's voice interrupted my rapture. "It's about time," he said. We chuckled in unison, knowing that time was not part of this dimension. I saw pictures of myself as a High Priestess of Grieving in Egypt, as an oracle in ancient Greece, as an Indian shaman. The pictures flowed from one to the other in time-lapse photography style.

Mike winked at me. "At last, you've got it," he declared. "Without me, there would have been no *you* as you are experiencing yourself right now. See? We are instruments for each other."

Although I had been swirled into a dance of the cosmos, I did not get dizzy. I was surefooted in space because there was nothing to stumble over. Then I heard Walter gently asking me if I would like to meet a special friend of his. I knew he was urging me to return from my trip, but I refused, saying, "I'm not ready."

The last image I had before joining Walter was of a luminous emerald in the shape of a seven-pointed star positioned between my eyes. Its pulse was swift and electrifying. It twinkled to the music of celestial spheres. I knew then that I did not have to rejoin the dance, because I *was* the dance. Walter gently helped me to my unsteady feet.

He guided me toward a full-length mirror and introduced me to myself. When I viewed my face in the mirror, I saw two huge eyes pulsating with pain, love, wisdom, and knowledge of my purpose as a healer. I felt as if I had been baptized. I saw myself as beautiful in my pain, in my love, and in my wisdom.

To everyone present I said, "The real test is whether you allow yourself to be in love with life, with yourself, and with others, because loving means letting go and re-divining."

Integrity and love have become my guidelines.

November 28, 1978

Since the acid trip, I have been stuttering over verb tenses. They don't make sense anymore. Divisions are illusory. I'm easily captivated by the sway of the trees, the journey of an ant, even water dribbling from a faucet. All things have a pulse of their own.

December 25, 1978

Could the truth be plainer? A blizzard this Christmas morning foiled our plans to visit Gil's parents, leaving the three of us awkwardly at home together, not knowing what to do. Kelli-Lynne and I snuggled under the Christmas tree and studied the blinking colored lights. After a while we both fell asleep. Kelli-Lynne dreamed about Mikey.

December 31, 1978

*A*nother year has ended, and a poem has come:

> *Love appears in many guises—*
> *The first flower of spring,*
> *A birth, a death,*
> *The fleeting glance of a stranger,*
> *The words of a familiar song*
> *You've never really listened to before.*
>
> *Family relationships taken for granted for decades,*
> *Where love appeared locked in . . .*
> *Until a chance event unites the whole,*
> *And each experiences the power and the mastery*
> *Of love and its beginnings.*

January 3, 1979

*O*ne of the members of the consciousness-raising group pointed out that I always "report to the group," rather than ask for help. I admitted to the offense and confessed that meeting every week for two and a half hours was too much for me, that my real desire was to make friends with solitude. I told the group that I did not want to lose their friendship by leaving. To prove my point, I agreed to return for one more meeting.

If I had been honest, I would have simply said that I am craving more time by myself. I often attempt to "make up" with people I assume I have hurt. When I get angry, I try to be nice. Glossing over a truth does not help me achieve my goals.

Persist, Rosie dear, persist. Learn your lessons of leaving.

January 18, 1979

*E*ager to learn more about my meetings with Mike, I decided to go an acidless music journey. I turned on some music and stretched out on the floor. Breathing deeply, I relaxed my body, emptied my mind of thoughts, and released my emotions. Within moments I was surprised to behold a dark radiant woman dressed in a monk's robe. Taking another deep breath, I saw that I was encased in a cocoon. My butterfly wings were moist. Voices warned me that it was too early to fly, yet the dark lady smiled with assurance, letting me know that the time was right for flying. I trusted her and knew I must be with her.

My gossamer body and new wings expanded and strengthened. Within seconds I was flying. I breathed in beauty, and as I did, the dark lady reminded me of the magic in ordinary realities. I understood immediately.

This robed woman embodied the essence of love, wisdom, and beauty. As I studied her features, her face transformed into that of Jesus Christ. Then she invited me to partake of "essence," but I was petrified of losing myself. Without effort, my butterfly body transformed into light, and Jesus extended his hands. They were the same hands I had seen in numerous dreams!

"Why me?" I questioned. I was not ready for this flood of light, and felt guilty about being unprepared.

Jesus turned back into the dark lady, and I danced with her—only now I was myself, and my hands exuded a healing light of their own. As I moved, I understood that I was an extension of a miraculous source of being. I danced in celebration—beckoning others to join me, ushering in life and newness, and knowing that all is light.

When the music ended, I wrote these words:

Healing returns energy to harmony.
I am the center of my own consciousness.
I need space to grow into my spaciousness.
I am at home with the universe.

January 20, 1979

I yearn to be receptive to transcendent wisdom. Pen in hand, I open my journal and invite my inner voice to guide me.

You are unlayering, and you are aligning yourself with your own creative spirituality. Wisdom resides within. Avoid being entrapped by involvements that lead you away from hearing and healing.

January 27, 1979

I have had little time to write this past week. I seem to be constantly searching for direction.

Allow your experience to voice the direction, rather then expecting the direction to voice your experience.

March 23, 1979

*T*oday is the second anniversary of Mike's death. Last year I waited for my parents and grandparents to come to my rescue. This year I sought to make peace with the twenty-third of March. The best approach, I reasoned, was to go into seclusion and remember Mike.

When a friend told me about a live-in community of Franciscan friars about 100 miles away, I decided to drive there for a retreat. I'd never been to a religious community before. Yet, the moment I entered the friary, I felt surrounded by a familiar ambiance, even though the residents addressed one another as "Father" or "Brother."

Upon my arrival, one of the fathers introduced himself and asked what I wanted to accomplish during my two-day stay.

"I've come to make a private retreat," I answered without thinking.

He nodded his head, smiled, and said, "In case you need guidance, I'm here."

"Thank you. I think I need to be by myself."

"Be easy with yourself, and remember, I'm here if you need spiritual direction," he repeated, and then pointed the way to my room.

I walked up the two flights of stairs, wondering what he meant by "spiritual direction." My room was small and furnished with only a bed, a sink, a desk, a chair, and a low, claw-footed bathtub. I could see the ocean waves from my window. I emptied my suitcase and placed a white candle and my journal on the desk.

Noticing that the ocean looked bluer than ever before, I decided to walk on the beach. There the subzero-degree winds and restless water revived me. Mike and I used to spend lots of time by the ocean, and now it holds his ashes, I mused, but we never frolicked on this particular beach.

"I'm a stranger here," I said out loud. "I don't know how to miss Mike at a place we never visited."

I walked on, trying to imagine him at my side. My hands were red and cold. I tripped over a rock and stumbled to my knees. "I can't make up a history we never had," I moaned. "I still don't know how to do this," I screamed at a seagull perched on a high rock. "I don't know how to remember Mike and be gentle with myself."

Returning to my room, I took a long bath. My windblown body prickled under the hot, soapy water. When my skin was well "pruned," I climbed out of the deep tub, wrapped myself in a towel, and reminded myself to go easy. After all, I had no telephone to answer, no meals to prepare, and no one to talk to. Yawning, I walked over to the bed and tested the firmness of the mattress. Then I curled up for a midmorning nap.

I woke up two hours later—too late for the 12:30 lunch. *Now* I can miss Mike, I told myself, but I didn't know how to bring on that state of being. So I got dressed and headed upstairs to see the art gallery.

No one was around. The oil paintings covering the walls were huge and brightly colored. As I strolled past them, I began moving my arms and feet in sweeping motions. My body responded to the light cascading through the window, and I traced the rays with my arms and legs.

Suddenly I was startled by the sound of someone clearing his throat. I stopped in my tracks.

"Are you a sister?" the man asked.

"No," I said with amusement.

"What are you doing here, besides dancing with my art?" he asked.

"I came here to grieve," I recited, careful to avoid looking in his direction. "This is the second anniversary of my son's death, and I need to be alone." I paused.

"I have some music you might be interested in," he told me. "In New Orleans they play jazz while carrying the bodies of the dead through the streets. Ever hear funeral jazz?"

"No," I whispered.

He placed a cassette in the tape recorder, turned the volume up, and walked out, saying, "The music is supposed to uplift those left behind. I'll be downstairs if you want to talk."

I strained to hear the beat. I normally don't like jazz, but for some reason I found the sharp, fast tempo exciting. After looking around to make sure nobody would surprise me again, I began moving to the rhythm of the music. My cheeks warmed; my hands and feet tingled. How could I explain that this dance was for Mike? Simple—there was no one to have to explain anything to, I reminded myself.

When my dance ended, I walked down to the first floor, avoiding the small chapel on the landing. I heard voices in the dining room, and avoided them too. I should never have told the artist my reason for being here, I groaned silently. What if he let everyone know?

To avoid more encounters, I returned to my room, put on my warm coat and mittens, and dashed back to the ocean. When my feet touched the sand, I looked up at the sun overhead and felt a surge of love for Mike well up in my heart. Aloud I said, "I love you, Mike. And I am sending you loving energy. That's what my dance was about." Then I ran freely along the short beach.

There by the ocean I understood that light is reflected love . . . and that love, in turn, is light. I flashed on the first Christmas after Mike died, when he had sent a sign of sunlight at Two Lights State Park. At the time, I did not grasp the full meaning of his act; only now did it make sense.

I returned to the friary refreshed, and excited that I had let myself go where I felt like going. I climbed the stairs to the art gallery—maybe to dance, maybe to look at the pictures, maybe to talk with the man who had interrupted my dance with his gift of music.

Entering the room, I saw the brother painting. He looked at me, and we giggled.

"Now we're even for walking in on each other's creativity," I said.

"Would you like to join me for a glass of wine?" he asked in a warm voice.

"I don't even know your name."

"Nor I, yours."

"Sure," I said. Last year, I had sipped wine alone, desperately trying to stop missing Mike. Now I loved him more, missed him a little less, and welcomed the idea of company. I saw an image of Mike as part of a universal light-dance, and I laughed.

Spirit cannot be understood
if it cannot be experienced.
One can only be spirit.
　　　　—Elisabeth Haich

Year Three

Intimacy, appreciation, sacredness, and playfulness—these are qualities I seek in others and in myself. The irony is that although I help other people release blocks that prevent them from exhibiting these aspects of themselves, I myself remain obstructed.

Does being grown-up mean settling for half-truths, mediocrity, and a life devoid of magic?

June 27, 1979

My reality is shifting. In the past whenever I asked for something, I felt inadequate and weak. In my family of origin, self-sufficiency reigned supreme. Now I am beginning to see that to be vulnerable is human. My perceptions change as I change, or is it the other way around? "I want my life to be my art," I confided to a friend.

Who I am at any moment changes.

July 10, 1979

A recurring dream invades my nights. I am driving a car across a high bridge. Suddenly, the car careens off the edge into the water below. I force the window open and watch in horror as the ocean creeps up to fill the inside of the car. I wait until the water is almost up to my nose, because I remember reading that a high water level creates a vacuum that allows the door of a submerged car to be opened. I wait impatiently, trying to conserve my energy and avoid panicking. I push against the door, and I hear a *whoosh* as it gives way. I wake up before I know whether or not I have surfaced.

When I imagine being a psychic instrument, I panic. I resist the idea of being a channel because I'm afraid I will have to sacrifice someone or something, and I refuse to give up more.

You may not have a choice.

August 6, 1979

The day after Kelli-Lynne's fifth birthday, I told Gil I wanted to separate. He wasn't surprised; nor was he interested in talking about logistics. I thought I would feel relieved, even exhilarated, but instead I dread informing our families of this decision.

The thought of not being a wife anymore is scary. Being a mother without being a wife is backward. Still, if marriage is a social solution to loneliness, I'll take the loneliness. The economic forecast for this coming winter is bleak, but is there ever a good time to strike out on one's own? Is there ever a time when leaving is easy?

A sense of failure hangs over me. I've never been a perfect wife, though I have tried. In the process, I almost sacrificed my spirit.

August 20, 1979

Our fourteenth anniversary was weird. Nothing felt right—neither acknowledging the occasion nor denying it. We still live together, but we have nothing to celebrate.

I am thankful for two dreams I had last night. In one, the words "holy, holy, holy" were chanted to me. The tones resonated throughout my body. At their conclusion, I half awoke, thinking that if I knew I was being propelled from the inside to become more holy, I would have more courage.

The "holy" chants were followed by a dream in which I was climbing a steep mountain. Two people on the summit were instructing me. One dropped down a rope and ordered me to tie it around my waist. Making the ascent by rope seemed too risky, so I looked around for an easier way. Unable to find a trail, I tied the rope securely around my waist and listened closely for more directions. I avoided looking down. As before, I awoke before I knew the outcome.

I am grieving again, only differently this time, I hurt, cry, talk to friends, and ask for help. I hide less. My parents remain unavailable to me.

August 25, 1979

I fight alone as my life is stripped of myths. The notion of family support has lost its power. Everyone in my family has uncried tears, unspoken frustrations, and unfulfilled dreams. I break the rules once again by stepping out of a familiar system that does not support my spirit and moving into an unknown future.

September 4, 1979

*A*t 9:47 this evening, I looked at the clock and knew that Liz, my adopted spiritual mother, had died. Trusting her wisdom about all that lay before her, I sent a surge of energy to encompass her spirit. As I stood in the middle of the kitchen crying, Gil walked in and asked what had was wrong. When I told him what had happened, he suggested calling Liz's husband to make sure. I didn't need to, I told him. I know what I know.

Already I miss Liz. Her death causes another shift in my life, for she had spent years surrounding me with unconditional love. In a meditation just last week, she appeared and offered me the gift of compassion. But now, when I need so badly to be touched, she is beyond my reach.

September 7, 1979

*A*s I glanced in the mirror early this Sunday morning, I saw that my eyes had taken up a large portion of my face. I looked like a rendering of Little Red Riding Hood the moment she realized a wolf was in her grandmother's bed. My eyes reflected fear and a haunting sadness.

The miracle is that although I have given in to layers upon layers of pain, my eyes have stayed open. Like the hero in D.H. Lawrence's *Sons and Lovers*, I will never stop searching for the one act of purity.

September 13, 1979

Today was the opening of a two-day healing workshop, and I'm already bored. This morning, when we started to talk of death, forgiveness, and the transformation that occurs in the healing process, the other group members quoted from books about grief. I spoke quietly about my suffering, and about the importance of living my life with spirit and love.

In the evening, I stayed alone in my room by the ocean. I sat naked in the small cabin, tracing the stars outside my window. With no other sounds in my midst, I had no trouble surrendering to the lulling of the waves. My final waking wish was to join with others who were not afraid to speak from the heart.

September 14, 1979

The leader of the workshop challenged us to answer the following questions: Where are you on your spiritual journey? When did you begin this period of healing?

I scanned memories of dreams for a beginning, but nothing came to my attention. Then I remembered a day about three months ago, when I engaged in a "role stripping" exercise. Attaching an order of importance to my identities as wife, mother, lover, friend, daughter, and healer, one by one I had let them go. "Daughter" was my sixth priority, and I imagined parting with that role and all the meaning it had for me. "Friend" was number five, a role I was saddened to release. It was painful to admit that "wife" was number four, but when I did, I felt relief, sadness, and fear. Mike's death prepared me to let go of "mother," next on the list, but what a struggle it was to let go of my maternal feelings. "Lover" followed. How dare I rank my role as lover above wife and mother, I thought, but I had given myself permission to be brutally honest during this exercise. Renouncing my role as healer—my number one priority—left me feeling hollow, as if my spirit had died. All that remained was stillness.

After reflecting on this activity, I wanted to be alone. I excused myself, assuring everyone in the group that I was okay. No sooner had I found a sunny spot on the lawn than the following poured out of me:

Be.
Be radiant.
Be still.
Be touched.
Be at peace.

A moment later another line appeared:

Love is forgiving. Forgiving precedes wholeness.

Someone had left crayons in the grass. Lifting the bright colors from between the blades of greenery, I turned to a blank page in my journal and began to color. The design that emerged reminded me of a stained glass window. When the drawing reached the edges of the page, I returned to the group, still role-less, yet refreshed.

Healing happens in the most unexpected ways. Endings . . . transitions. If only I could believe my journey *outside* the workshop will end in transformation.

After I returned home, Kelli-Lynne and I walked on the beach, holding hands and chattering as we searched for sea glass. My feelings for her have no strings attached. I love her for who she is, not for who I might want her to be. I want for her what I want for myself: honesty, love, humor, and movement with purpose

October 19, 1979

My mother called today, and I told her I will be moving out in one week. I explained that I would be house-sitting in another part of town for a month while looking for a place of my own.

"Are you happy?" she asked.

How can I be happy with so many endings? If I were happy, I reasoned silently, I would not be moving. Unknowns close in on me and my mother wants to know if I'm happy.

Once again she asked, "But are you happy?"

"Mom, I'm doing what I need to do. I have chosen to live, and now I am trying hard to create an honest life that will *justify* my decision to live."

Silence. Then she said, "Good, because it's your life."

I replied, "You're right. And I am living it in my own way, which is different from your way. This is what I must do in order to live." I didn't tell her why; she would never understand my need to behold myself.

∞ ∞

November 2, 1979

Moving day! If it is true that who you are depends on what you are feeling, I am a multilayered collage.

As I settled into my temporary shelter, I looked with interest at the treasures I had chosen to bring with me: a few candles, several books, many plants, a print of the Desiderata words "I am a child of the universe," my zither, and a candle Mike had hand-dipped for me when he was fourteen years old.

Earlier in the day I had taken a long walk on the beach that spreads for miles in front of the house. The water was healing. I asked for a sign that I was on the right track, and immediately I stumbled over a heart-shaped rock. I chanted, "Listen, listen, listen, to my heart's song. / Listen, listen, listen to my heart's song. / I will never forget you, I will never forsake you. . . ." After that, I felt more at home than I had in years.

This evening, Kelli-Lynne chose her bedroom. We filled it with her toys and stuffed animal friends. Then she skipped about, exploring the house and asking questions—she's still trying to make sense of all this. Soon afterward, I read her a bedtime story, we cuddled, and I tucked her in bed, leaving a small night-light on and assuring her I would be sleeping in the next room. Then I built a fire to keep us warm, and settled into the unfamiliar living room couch, exhausted.

Here I am, thirty-five and a half years old and on my own for the first time in my life. I am creating a new world for my daughter and me. As I watch the blaze in the fireplace, I wonder how she will look back on this portion of her life. Most of all, I wonder if I am being fair to her.

While arranging her room, I had explained to Kelli-Lynne that I left her dad because I was not happy.

She replied, "*I* was, so why did you have to take *me* away, too?"

"Good question," I commented. Surprising myself, I added, "Because I am your mother, and we belong together."

Actually, of course, Kelli-Lynne belongs to both Gil and me. We have agreed that she will spend most of the week with me because Gil works weekdays from eight to five. He will have her on weekends. The plan sounds reasonable, but what will be its impact on Kelli-Lynne? Too tired to think anymore, I relax, letting the sizzling coals warm my face and feet while fantasizing about the sounds of the cosmos lulling me to sleep.

November 9, 1979

*T*o mark the end of week number one on my own, I bought lemon bath beads and a loofah sponge. Then I created a ritual of immersion—a bathtub filled with water so hot I had to wait ten minutes before stepping into it.

One major accomplishment this week consisted of asking for a raise and more teaching hours at the university. I was surprised at how easy it was to assert myself. I was even more surprised by the answer: *yes!*

Last night I dreamed that I was driving to a place I had never been before. The traveling was smooth until I made a ninety-degree turn onto a slippery, snow-covered road. I asked a man for directions, whereupon he pointed to the icy road. I took a deep breath and continued on in the darkness. Each day is like driving along a slippery road, and I am determined to learn the rules of driving under adverse conditions.

November 18, 1979

*K*elli-Lynne crawled into my bed at four o'clock this morning. She curled her body next to mine, and we slept like two puppies.

I am responsible for having physically walked out of a marriage. I carry the burden of having ended a relationship that did not provide for my spirit. Looking at Kelli-Lynne's little-girl face and listening to her breathe, I felt my love for her. I trust that we will do the best we can.

December 1, 1979

*A*nother move—this time, into my own apartment. With a little help from my friends, I loaded and transported furniture, dishes, more books, lamps, furniture and more toys for Kelli-Lynne, spices, and picture albums. By sunset I was in. Familiar furnishings now surround me.

I sit on the cozy pillow couch, gazing at the stars. How quiet everything is tonight! And how proud I am to have so quickly created a home out of these four rooms.

December 3, 1979

*K*elli-Lynne and I spent most of the day arranging her bedroom. She told me where she wanted each of her treasures, including her toy box and every one of her stuffed animal companions. I hung curtains while she groped to make her bed. I put her clothes in drawers as she arranged her books. We both giggled upon discovering that we don't own a clock and that neither of us has ever worked a gas stove. Kelli-Lynne wondered if the house would creak in the night, if spirits would be in her closet, and if Mikey would know where we lived now that we both had new rooms. I caught my breath. I had been so busy that I hadn't thought about Mike.

December 21, 1979

Although Gil has been separated from me these past seven weeks, he has not been separated from my family. In fact, everyone in the family has fantasies about us getting back together. I'm tired of trying to please others at the expense of meeting my own needs.

December 25, 1979

This was the third Christmas without Mike and my first as a single mom. Christmas Eve at my parents' house was a blur. I focused my attention on Kelli-Lynne and her two cousins. I stroked my sheer black satin dress to remind myself that I was sane. At the end of the evening, I packed up my gifts and bundled them into the car, missing Kelli-Lynne even before backing out of the driveway. I had agreed with Gil that she would be happier spending the traditional Christmas day with his family, but I was wretched leaving my daughter on a holiday, especially now.

I had to stop at the side of the road twice during the eight-mile drive to my apartment, for I was unable to see through my tears. I know the untangling has only begun.

January 12, 1980

I'm so often pushing, seldom affirming what I've accomplished, and further complicating the cycle by chiding myself about all that remains to be done. This week, for a change, I have eased up.

Living alone is right for now. I am learning to befriend myself, to grant myself time, patience, and the freedom to make mistakes. I have discovered from experiences gained in tragedy that I deserve peace without a price. For the first time in my life, I feel the whisperings of integrity.

The quest for the Holy Grail begins within.

Actually, I have been discovering a great deal. I used to feel sacredness and sensuality as separate forces within me. As a result, I felt compelled to abide by either one or the other. Now I understand that spirituality can be a passionate pursuit, and passion can be a spiritual feeling. In choosing one, I choose the other.

The only way backward or forward is through yourself.

Truths pour onto the page. But how, I wonder, can grief be inspirational? Whether it is or isn't, I have had enough of it. I have survived more endings in the last three years than many people experience in a lifetime. I want to toss grief in the closest Goodwill box, just as I drop in clothing that no longer fits. How desperately I want to boast that I have outgrown grief.

To feel is to heal.

January 13, 1980

I feel like the delicate placenta of my unconscious has ruptured and I am being lubricated by creative waters. I shiver in recognition of yet another limiting belief: I will have to give up something else. "I have paid enough," I wail to the walls of my apartment. "I have given up my ovaries, my son, my marriage, my illusions. What else *is* there?" I keep myself mediocre to avoid more tragedy.

Self-defeating behavior is being exorcised.

Already I can see that this is not a reenactment of the winter of my discontent. This is the winter of the planting of seeds.

January 14, 1980

I've had my straight hair curled in a permanent wave. Each time I catch a glimpse of myself in a mirror, I look again. I seem to have put more "elf" in myself. The woman and the unknown creative child within me are becoming allies.

January 17, 1980

A sleepless night. At about three o'clock this morning, I recalled the words of a Gestalt therapist who said, "If you can't sleep, get up and start working on what you have been avoiding." With a groan, I got up and started writing. I began with two lines:

> *I don't want to work simply to make money.*
> *I want to teach and reach people at a very deep level.*

Then I sighed, fully facing my quandary. I need to make money, and I need to feel purposeful. Teaching assertiveness training classes to uninterested college students, I concluded, is not purposeful.

Can a person be angry and powerful at the same time? Intellectually, I know that withholding emotion causes a stumbling block in the grieving process, and yet I have learned to be ashamed of my anger. Now I'm in the middle of another cycle of mourning, and until I can acknowledge my anger without putting myself down for making a scene, I won't be able to feel anything else. Once again, I die to old family myths while reinventing new ones for Kelli-Lynne and me.

I can appreciate why Kelli-Lynne sucks her thumb. I just tried it, but my teeth got in the way.

January 28, 1980

I am forced to change or shrink. Yearning to retain some of my optimism and innocence, I collapsed into the pillow couch this morning and sobbed. I haven't the energy to support my own body. I feel haunted by my mother's prediction that I would have a mental or physical breakdown after Mike's death. If I have to break down in order to break through, then damn it, I will! I will not allow *anyone* to control how much I feel, I asserted, not even me. I struck out at the pillows, as if to expel my mother's prediction.

I cried deeply and loudly, losing myself in my tears—even my feet trembled. My anguish would have been more muted had I not known that I was born to make a difference. As it was, I held to three guiding truths: my light is important, my *life* is important, and my soul will not be ransomed.

My body continued to shake as I tried to make sense of the turmoil. Gasping for breath, I recalled early memories of physical punishment. Convinced at the time that I deserved the spankings, I had no choice but to lean over and take them. Now, I decided, was a perfect time to breathe life into my heart and soul.

After thirty-five years, I am finding my direction. I am recovering truths and rhythms of my own. Sometimes I am angry that I have to do this alone, but I vow never to turn back.

January 30, 1980

I awoke this morning with traces of a dream about my grandfather. Bomp was preparing me for his death. He told me of the family's "narrow understanding," of his connection with me through our "expanded awareness," and of his promise to maintain this link after his death. "I will field you," he said simply, and in the dream I understood the meaning of his words.

I got out of bed knowing that Bomp's body was worn out and that he could not accept the healing I had been sending him. I, of course, wanted him to live, for he had always has been a key figure in my life; he had named his three boats after me, and I had named my daughter after him. Making my way to the telephone, I vowed to respect his destiny, to avoid selfishly trying to hold him here, and to send him energy to use for his own purposes—even for strengthening his intention to die, if need be.

Around nine o'clock, I called and spoke to Bomp, my voice hushed and serious. He said, "I was not in my body for the last two nights. I was somewhere else, visiting with Mike and you, and I didn't want to return to my body. I wanted to stay with Mike, but he told me it was not yet time."

Bomp also said that Mike had commented on how much he loved both of us. I breathed fully, appreciating the clarity of this report.

"I know I am almost ready to die, and I need to talk to you," he added. "Then I can rest."

Responding to the urgency in his voice, I drove out to see him. He was glad I had come. After pledging ourselves to confidentiality, we spent hours speaking from our depths.

February 1, 1980

Taking care of myself was my top priority today. I removed the telephone from the hook. Then I filled the tub with hot water and bubble bath, took a bath, washed my hair, and listened to music. I repotted plants and played in the oozy mud. I also made chicken soup, mindful of Carl Simonton's advice: Identify what you do for yourself when you are sick, then do these things for yourself *before* you get sick. I dragged out the warm quilt, propped myself up with pillows, sipped some chicken soup, and wrote these lines:

> *Deliver me from always being strong.*
> *Deliver me from always putting others first.*
> *Deliver me from always looking to others for insight.*
> *Deliver me from settling for mediocrity.*
> *Deliver me from my past.*

After setting down my pen, I had a profound realization. I recognized that I am my *own* deliverer!

February 2, 1980

𝓘 had a shake-up dream earlier this evening. I was shopping in an exclusive department store overseas and needed to get to the third floor. The only way up was through a narrow white tunnel. I remarked, "How odd that in such a fine store there is no elevator."

I was with a woman who knew how to reach the third floor. Although I relied on her navigating skills, the passageway was familiar to me. When we approached the end of the tunnel, the third floor was in sight, but the only access to it was by way of a trapeze. Someone behind me offered to give me a slight push to gain momentum. My woman friend, however, signaled me to push her first; I did, and she landed on the third floor. By then, the person behind me had gone, and I was stranded. I mounted the trapeze, hooked up the safety clasp, and flipped upside down, surprised that I was not terribly frightened. Then somebody appeared and gave me a push, but it was too gentle. Two more pushes brought me closer each time, but not close enough. Frustrated at having to rely on anyone for assistance, I realized that I could gain motion by using my legs. I swung them, pumped higher, and woke up!

If dreams are messages from the soul, what does my soul want me to know? It seems to be informing me that I can provide my own momentum, and that as long as the safety clasp is in place, seeing the world upside down is not scary. Who is this mysterious "someone" offering to push me? Do I dare to trust the unseen, the invisible?

I have had so many dreams about bridges, tunnels, and other narrow passageways. Might these structures represent "birth tunnels" to other dimensions, other realities? I seem to be bridging worlds and, unaided by road maps, relying entirely on direct experience.

February 5, 1980

*K*elli-Lynne crept into my bed this morning, and we cuddled. I asked if she could remember any dreams. She said no. I told her I had had a dream about two seals frolicking in the water. Suddenly, they got beached. They washed up on shore, and people stared at them, but nobody helped them back into the water. Kelli-Lynne's face lit up, and she invited me to be a playful seal with her. We "sealed," and even took a "seal bath" together so we could give my dream a happy ending.

Yesterday, while listening to the radio, I heard a minister say, "What is important is not death, but rather the meaning we attach to it." Even though Mike has been dead for three years, he continues to exchange living energy with me. By day, I miss him; in nighttime dreams and visits, I am in touch with him. I have been sentenced to one reality, and my soul speaks of another—a "multidimensional consciousness" I could not have known were it not for the death of my son.

February 28, 1980

I bought a flowering baby's breath plant today, an early birthday gift for myself. I prefer flowers to food because they feed so many organs at once, especially the nose, eyes, and heart. Upon my return home, I called some friends and invited them to my birthday party on the third of March. I felt arrogant gifting myself in these ways. I am far more comfortable encouraging others to indulge themselves.

I draw on the moon for power even though I no longer experience the monthly cycles. I've stopped taking the estrogen pills, so I'm plunged into hot flashes at night, soaking the bed. I tried ginseng, but that didn't help. I tried visualizing hot flashes as orgasms, but my imagination was not sufficiently fantasy oriented. I called three gynecologists, each of whom said to take the estrogen for seventeen more years. Am I the only woman who resents taking synthetic hormones from a bottle that lists cancer as a side effect?

*M*y thirty-sixth birthday party was indeed a celebration. In honor of myself, I wore my long red dress and put a fresh rose in my hair. Glancing in the full-length mirror, I noticed how attractive I looked. Thirty-six and beautiful! "It's about time," I said, smiling at the echo of the words Mike had spoken during my acid trip.

Friends arrived in festive clothes. No matter which room I was in, I was greeted with hugs. After a while everyone gathered in the living room, someone turned off the lights, and Kelli-Lynne came in carrying a huge chocolate cake ablaze with thirty-six candles. I invited her to help me quell the flames. Only after we had successfully blown out all the candles did I realize that I had forgotten to make a wish. No matter—I had everything I wanted right here in one room.

Happiness of this sort is new for me. After Mike was killed, I never thought I'd be celebrating anything, certainly not my birthday.

*A*nother night has kept me wet and awake. I used to think I was immune to hot flashes because I was a feminist. But no, I struggle even in sleep. Earlier this week I dreamed about karma, past lives, and endings. I don't know what "karmic debt" means, but I have a hunch that is exactly what I am facing.

I awoke to a dark, sleeting day that for some reason filled me with dread. I felt like Cassandra, prophet of tragedy. The telephone interrupted my morbid thoughts. It was a friend saying that the consciousness-raising group would be meeting as planned because the roads weren't bad. Then I realized that the gloom surrounding me was related to the upcoming anniversary of Mike's death. On the dark, wet March day of his death, school had been canceled and the consciousness-raising group had not. On this dark day, I felt too vulnerable to go to group, but I went anyway, for it no longer made sense to deprive myself of support.

This time I spoke first. I told how cut off I had been feeling; reviewed questions I had been entertaining about past lives and karmic debts; and confessed that I was still missing Mike. I complained freely without once apologizing for taking too much time. Friends hugged me, and I cried. Never before had I allowed myself to draw comfort from this group!

When I returned to my apartment, floods of convulsive sobs tore through my body—salty old tears from long, long ago. I sobbed for the losses I had sustained and for the small child who, buried within me, had always felt lonely and separated. The more I cried, the more clearly I could see that desperate six-year-old child escaping to the darkness of her large closet, where she would curl up alone for hours. I used to gravitate between being afraid someone would discover me there and being terrified no one would miss me. I always came out on my own, more convinced than ever that I didn't matter.

On the heels of my tears came insights. When I get scared, I'm six years old again; I withdraw, no longer to my closet but to a place of silence and aloneness. Nurturing the orphaned child within is my responsibility now. At the same time I am a mother to my own six-year-old daughter—a child who questions and wonders, who feels and appreciates her own magic. In so many ways, our children show us new possibilities.

March 18, 1980

Last night I slept soundly for the first time in three weeks. I was exhausted from giving in to the pain I'd been shadow-boxing with for so long. Opening my eyes in the morning, I was astounded by how refreshed and light I felt. I do believe that I am more than a survivor—I am a builder!

Peer supervision this morning was at my apartment. After everyone left, I became obsessed with the filthy hallways of this building. Each time I walk through them, I grimace, hold my nose, and run as fast as I can to get to my floor without feeling contaminated by the odor of cat urine. Embarrassed that my friends had to walk through this filth to get to me, and tired of waiting for the landlords to clean it up, I swept with fury, clearing away six months' worth of garbage and cat shit. When I was finished, my face was filthy, and my hair white with plaster dust. I looked like a chimney sweep, but I had at least taken action instead of complaining.

March 20, 1980

*K*elli-Lynne just asked me if days are squares or circles. Only a child would wonder about such things. I asked her what she thought, and she said, "Both." So we sat down to draw our versions of a circle day and a square day. I would like a spiral day!

March 23, 1980

*O*nce again, I hide away at the friary to mark this day of transition for my son. Here I can see clearly that I am my sole distraction. When I turn to writing, sentences appear like magic on the paper.

To be vulnerable is to be godlike.

Transitions create openings.

Openings are opportunities to release energy.

Releasing heralds essence.

I shiver in response to the prayerful words, suddenly realizing that I have not prayed since Mike's death. From somewhere deep inside, I am acutely aware that my soul is an individualized expression of my essence, which is precisely what I have been trying to recover. Is it also true that my essence has been trying to claim me?

The mystery is the magic. True celebration springs from love.

I admit that when I fill with love, I become an offering—which is nothing like being an orphan.

With intention, I breathe in and out, filling my body and then the entire room with love. In the process, I sense the stirrings of reverence. I hug myself, nurturing my sacredness and remembering my beginnings. Sitting down once again, I write:

> *I began in beauty.*
> *I began in love.*
> *I began in light.*

As I reinvest in my essence, I become aware of an indwelling faith that everything will happen in its proper time. With expanded clarity, I continue to write:

> *I am my own book. I am the plot. I am reflected in each of the characters. I create the conflict. I live the themes. I am the moral of the story. I decide if I am fiction or nonfiction, mystery or tragedy or Gothic romance.*

At this moment, I fully understand how complicated it was for Mike to have been my son, and for me to have been his mother. We were teachers for each other, yet we refused to learn from each other. Somehow the roles of mother and son prevented us from revealing our essences until death intervened.

Grief is reverence in disguise.

I am nurtured here by silence and space. The ocean soothes me; people are nearby in case I crumble; the chapel quiets my heart. I have succeeded in convincing most people that my life is in control. Here, however, it is safe to cry the unwept tears. I don't need answers; feelings will do. I have a treasure chest within that is filled with love.

March 24, 1980

During the night, I had severe chest pains. I felt as if my heart were being chiseled open. Each time I surrender to my feelings, my heart aches. I expect to feel the lightness of relief, but I feel only pain. Parts of me that no longer serve a purpose seem to dissolve as my defenses crumble, but why all the pain?

Being cloistered here at the friary attunes me to a gentle rhythm. I no longer slow down by getting sick. Nor do I strive to hide behind grief. I know that passion is the opposite of grief, but I do not feel passionate, not yet.

This morning I wandered into the chapel, as if pulled by a magnet. I knelt on the floor, folded my hands, breathed a long sigh, and said aloud, "God, I forgive you for my son's death." A surge of relief flashed through me. My face was wet with tears. I breathed deeply, shocked by the force that had traveled through me. The power of forgiveness was orgasmic. I bowed my head and received waves of light.

Leaving the sanctuary, I stepped outside to dance in the open air. I swirled, my hands uplifted, tears running down my face, my heart throbbing, and my feet responding to the simple rhythms of my soul. I danced until I could no longer stand. When I returned to the friary, one of the priests held out his arms and embraced me. He didn't say a word. I knew, nevertheless, that he had witnessed my dance.

Sacredness . . . forgiveness . . . love. Love is for-giving. No wonder my heart felt chiseled open last night! How else could I have prepared for such a moment? These three years I have secretly blamed God for the death of my son. How freeing it is to let go again. There is always an again.

Yes—until your soul has accepted its fullness.

A life that is truly lived is constantly burning away the veils of illusion, gradually revealing the essence of the individual.
                —Marion Woodman

Year Four

I smile and shake my head over conversations I've had with my almost six-year-old daughter. "Are you going to get married when you grow up?" she asked while we were setting the table for dinner.

"Probably," I responded. "What's 'grown up,' anyway?"

"It's when you know who you want to marry, and you don't have to ask your mother and father if you can," she said without hesitation.

I looked at her with a straight face and told her I wasn't "grown up" yet.

Later, as she was drying the silverware, she noticed some abstract sketches I had made at the friary. She asked what they meant.

"I don't know," I told her. "They are just drawings about what I was feeling."

She studied the sketches, then asked if I would like her to tell me what they meant. Very seriously, she explained that the first sketch was of a panther spirit which, like all animal spirits, is different from people spirits.

"How are panther spirits and people spirits different?" I inquired.

"People spirits are different sizes. An adult's spirit is shaped like an O and is surrounded by forty shoots. A teenager's is a smaller O with twenty shoots, and a baby's is a small dot with no shoots. When you get

131

to be eighty, your shoots are different colors. But animals have no shoots, just like baby people."

She spoke with the voice of authority. Curious, I asked where she had learned this.

"I've always known about spirits. I learned it a long, long time ago," she replied.

"I'm glad you remembered," I said.

April 6, 1980

I am feeling more determined to be divorced than I ever imagined I would. Yet, accompanying this determination is grief . . . again. A fourteen-year marriage is over. Mike was fourteen when he died. Do I live my life in fourteen-year cycles?

April 25, 1980

*S*pring is here. I miss our old neighborhood by the ocean. I remember the sounds of the local kids as they bounded through the three adjacent yards that formed one large playground. The children and I spent hours in our tire swing making up stories about the shapes of the passing clouds. Now I feel guilty about uprooting Kelli-Lynne. Here there are no trees, no ocean, no children to play with—not even a yard.

She deserves more, and I do, too. Daring to act on my integrity has cost me a lifestyle. Although the first warm breaths of spring cause me to miss the natural order, simplicity, and beauty of the old neighborhood, I don't regret my decision to divorce.

May 3, 1980

*G*il called today, saying he wanted to talk. I drove to "his" house and joined him for supper. Afterward I looked at him and told him I hoped I hadn't hurt his spirit. He was embarrassed. I explained that the divorce meant I was acknowledging a mistake I had made, but I refused to accept full blame for a marriage that did not work out. He nodded.

Tomorrow would have been Mike's eighteenth birthday. Later in the month he would have graduated from high school. By then I want to have graduated from this marriage.

When I got home, Kelli-Lynne invited me into her bedroom. She told me she had been crying because she was missing Mike. I held her tightly, and we cried together. She asked me to describe what Mike had looked like, but before I started, she blurted out, "I can't remember what Mikey's *voice* sounded like." She was trembling. "How old would Mikey be on his birthday?"

"Eighteen," I told her.

"Last year I made a birthday cake for him. Do you remember?"

"Yes, I remember. It had blue decorations and white frosting, and it was chocolate inside."

"He would have liked it."

"Yes," I agreed.

"I'm not making a cake for him this year, you know, because he can't eat it anyway. But I need to do something so I won't keep forgetting his voice."

"Maybe we could plant flowers in the community garden. Then when they begin to grow, we can remember Mike together. You know, Kelli-Lynne," I said gently, "I cannot remember very clearly how Mikey's voice sounded, either."

"Does that mean we don't love him as much?" she wanted to know.

"No, it means that I remember times we spent together more than what his voice sounded like."

"Me, too. And that's okay—right, Mom?"

"Yes, Pumpkin. That's okay."

We rocked each other until she asked, "Can we make some popcorn now? Mike loved popcorn."

"Of course," I replied, also feeling a sudden craving for popcorn.

May 4, 1980

ike's birthday and Mother's Day coincided this year. To celebrate, Kelli-Lynne and I went to Mackworth Island for a picnic lunch. There she made two sand cakes: one for me and one for Mike. The bittersweetness of her culinary intentions brought tears to my eyes.

May 20, 1980

I've often heard people speak of scaring the hell out of someone. What would I be like if *heaven* were scared *in?* Is that what praying is all about?

In my most recent dream, I was wandering around in a familiar house. I opened a partially hidden door and walked into a large sunlit room. A small forest of plants curtained each window. Appreciating the time and care that had been dedicated to these blooms, I wanted to meet the gardener. Then I noticed a long mahogany table that supported several cactus plants growing without soil or pots. Someone had planned this room very carefully, I concluded, and I knew I belonged here.

Immediately upon waking, I remembered the mangy cactus plant Mike had bought for me—the only plant I felt comfortable placing on his coffin in the funeral home. Is Mike sending me dreams? Is he the gardener? Does he tend my soul? What would it mean for *me* to be the gardener of my soul?

In another dream, I drove a car into a parking lot in front of the house I grew up in. The engine accelerated, and each time I tightened my grip on the steering wheel, the motor speeded up even more. I slammed on the brakes, but that did not help. I yanked my keys from the ignition, but the car speeded on. I figured I had no choice but to stay behind the wheel, steering the runaway car. A man came over from the sidewalk and counseled me, "Loosen your grip on the steering wheel. You are wasting your energy." As I relaxed my grip, the motor slowed down.

Certainly my life has accelerated, and I pride myself on being in the driver's seat. Most recently, I've been directing a great deal of energy toward earning money. But who was the man advising me to loosen my grip? I did not recognize him, yet I trusted his advice.

May 29, 1980

*I*n last night's dream, I was a captive in a prisoner-of-war camp. A camp official drove up in a long black car and demanded to know who had a son named Mike with a last name I couldn't quite understand. No one responded. I said I had a son named Mike Hall. He marched me off to a narrow room, where a guard offered me money if I would sign my son over to her. I was furious! "I will die before I do that," I told her. "I may be a prisoner, but I do have some power."

Later in the dream, I was one of several prisoners herded outside to a large enclosure filled with animals. A guard ordered us to watch as the animals were slaughtered one by one. I managed to hide two lambs under my long skirt. I awoke feeling as though I had won a huge victory.

June 6, 1980

$\mathscr{I}$ am at Monhegan Island, about twenty-seven miles from the mainland, to escape from what would have been Mike's high school graduation. For the past several weeks, each time I picked up a newspaper and saw articles about commencement, I felt battered, as though Mike's death had happened yesterday. I was not prepared for such intense pain, or for the jealousy I felt toward families with living graduates.

Here there are no newspapers, no schools, no cars, no electricity, no clocks—only the ocean, birds, deer, flowers, and a big sky. Today we had a giant thunderstorm. For an instant, all of nature seemed to hold its breath; then heavy raindrops fell, and nature roared. Mike would have loved it here.

The blast of a foghorn punctuates my thoughts. Looking out the window of my small cottage, I can see the white-capped ocean and small boats assaulted by the winds and driving rains. With my eyes, I trace the path of raindrops whipped off the eaves by the wind. I see their beginnings, and I follow their descents as they disappear into a puddle. I try to experience them as raindrops again, but cannot. Their evolution seems guided by the irreversible principle of formation–descent–absorption.

Closing my eyes I see a sudden spark of light. For a moment, it exists on its own, then it commingles sometimes with the darkness and other times with the light. The spark—like the raindrops—takes form, then merges, giving rise to a new configuration. Is this merging a reality or an optical illusion?

As you merge, you emerge.

June 22, 1980

$\mathscr{H}$urrah! I am a colleague in the Creative Education Foundation. The board of trustees at CPSI, where I teach for five days each year, has recognized me as a contributor to the field of creativity. Now I have a diploma—a distinction I was unable to acquire earlier in my life.

June 25, 1980

I am sitting alone on "my mountain" contemplating wizardry. Somehow I know that wizards gift one another with creative intimacy. Furthermore, I can recognize a wizard when I see one, because "openings" appear spontaneously in the surrounding energy field. Where did this information come from? How long have I been aware of it?

Forever. But you have only recently made a decision to practice your powers.

I do know that wizards are grounded in nature's principles and that they create openings because they know where the interfaces are between dimensions. But I do not know if wizards are initiated.

June 26, 1980

I've learned a new lesson in trust. I used to trust naively, become disillusioned, then feel hurt. Now I am more discerning. I give equal attention to the voices of reason and intuition. Perhaps that is what "seasoned trust" is all about.

June 27, 1980

*W*hile teaching and learning at CPSI, I trust my direction. I feel grounded in experience, the seedbed that underlies conceptual knowing. Perhaps because of this mooring, I realize that my job is to enjoy life. I have been humming the verse "'Tis a gift to be simple, 'tis a gift to be free / 'Tis a gift to come 'round where we ought to be. . . ," aware from a deep place within that healing occurs when personality has changed.

July 3, 1980

I resolve to relocate by September, when Kelli-Lynne starts school. I envision a house with a yard and at least one tree.

Many of my dreams these past few nights have been about teaching. I am either showing people how to see auras or speaking of refracted light.

August 30, 1980

*M*oving day—my third in ten months. This one has taken me out of the apartment and into my own house. No more moves, I tell myself, unable to imagine what permanence would even look like.

I feel exhausted from hundreds of trips up and down the three flights of stairs, and I was not even the one lugging the heavy furniture! While making the last swing around the four rooms of the apartment to be sure nothing would be left behind, I spotted something lying in the middle of the dining room floor: it was a photograph of Mike. Earlier, my file cabinet drawer wouldn't close because a folder of Mike's poems was in the way. And so, he resides with me still.

September 1, 1980

*T*he new house is such a gift. I even enjoy washing clothes here, because after I hang them outside, they smell like fresh air and grass. The chirping crickets lull me to sleep at night and awaken me in the morning.

Now I will be able to see the changing colors of trees in front of the house. I will be able to feel the transitions from season to season, and my own transitions as well.

My mother called today. In the course of our conversation, she referred to Kelli-Lynne as her number one grandchild—a comment that both angered and saddened me. She seems to deny Mike's existence as readily as she rejects my life choices.

October 10, 1980

I have at last rented an office. The lease expires in a year, and the rent is reasonable because the building is to be renovated. My primary goal is to promote myself as a therapist. I'm also busy teaching a course entitled The Psychology of Self-Image, which I codesigned.

October 15, 1980

*T*hank God for movement! I opened a credit card account today, *in my own name.*

When Kelli-Lynne came home from school, she looked me straight in the eye and said, "You know, Mom, Mike was one-half responsible for his own death, because he should have known not to go near the downed wire."

I gulped, prepared to plead his case. Why did I think I had to defend my dead son when Kelli-Lynne had spoken the truth?

Then she remarked that I should have told him not to go out. I sighed and reminded her that I had told him to be careful.

She went on to say she had been discussing Mike's death with one of her friends at school, and her friend had asked if *she* felt responsible. "How could I?" she replied. "I was only two and a half years old!"

October 16, 1980

*A*n evening at the symphony caused my barriers to crumble, I cried through several passages. Live music is tribute and celebration. How have I managed to be without it for so many years?

It was not safe to feel touched, that's all.

October 27, 1980

A draft of the divorce decree arrived from Gil's lawyer. Having expected a fair agreement, I was disappointed.

I read somewhere recently that life consists of merging, separating, and individuating, and that a psychic reorganization takes place each time we complete one of these stages. After a year of separation with no divorce, I feel like I am being held back from this reorganization. In the meantime, I seem to be repeating the grief cycle of *denial* (I want to be fair, so Gil and I can be friends and cooperate in this divorce), *anger* (at Gil, his lawyer, my lawyer, and myself, for drawing out this process), and *bargaining* (negotiating for eleven months and seeing no changes except in my bank account). I want to be unmarried!

November 6, 1980

I long to see with the eyes of my dreams. In last night's first episode, I was sitting in a square wooden box that resembled a child's swing. But instead of swinging, I was learning to fly. As long as I relaxed, my ascents and descents were calm. I must learn how to relax in waking life, and to fly toward my soul.

In the second dream, I was translating poetry from spirit to matter. I had to listen intently, yet in a relaxed manner. I agreed, in the end, to write a poem entitled "The Eyes of the Soul."

The swing dream is not my first one about propelling myself higher; nor is the translating dream the first about writing. Dare I believe that I am being prepared for some kind of breakthrough?

November 11, 1980

Last night's dreams were uniquely physical. In the first one, I was observing my body and noticed a tube attached to my pubic bone. It looked like a penis, only it was filled with blood. I understood that I was about to begin menstruating, and that I could detach the penis and use it as a tampon. "After all, it is my birthright," I announced, giggling at my ingenuity.

I woke up wondering what Freud would do with this dream. Would he consider it expressive of an integration of my masculine and feminine aspects?

Later in the night, I dreamed I was in the labor room of a hospital. I was preparing to give birth, and wanted to be alone. I watched with interest as I gave birth to a multicolored kitten. Smugly, I thought, "People will be so surprised!"

These dreams make perfect sense to me. I am in labor, and I do welcome the unexpected. Their guidance, however, is paradoxical: on a physical level I want to exert control, especially with regard to the divorce, while on a spiritual level I want to fly, translate ethereal poetry, and give birth. I shared the surprise kitten dream with a friend, who remarked casually, "Some people believe that kittens and cats are symbolic of the feminine, the intuitive," and we both smiled.

November 21, 1980

The lessons are always about love. What matters is only what you give with love. Love is for giving.

Mike's death has splintered my family. He tried to teach us about love, tried to heal and unify the family, but his voice was too little to be heard.

I am here. In the stillness I reside. And my voice is heard by you. The rightness of my teachings reside within you, for we are linked in love. In the future our voices will become blended.

At thirty-six, I struggle to be big enough to be heard, and yet I know I cannot change my family. They are not the perfect parents; nor am I the perfect daughter.

Speak where you will be listened to. Words of truth are precious to those who are ready for them. Do not judge yourself by family receptivity. Your field extends well beyond family, as does mine. Remember your original intent to serve. Service is never limited to the few. Serve those who seek further understanding.

December 5, 1980

I resigned today from teaching psychology to first-year college students. Once again I have learned the difference between giving people what they need as opposed to what they want. The day I typed my letter of resignation, I was offered three contracts to teach stress management workshops. I will be working less and earning more!

December 9, 1980

Attending another four-day Body-Centered Psychotherapy workshop inspired me to change some of my patterns of defending myself. According to Ron Kurtz, the leader, completion is always waiting to happen; *our* task to is intervene at choice points, which is where the options are. Either we defend our cherished ways of resisting by protecting ourselves at these choice points, or we reach out and risk a different, more nourishing way of being.

When Ron asked for a volunteer, I took the risk because I felt safe with him. I told him that when I relax, I feel like crying, and that to avoid being overwhelmed by my tears, I defend myself by looking strong and in control.

"I will keep you from breaking down," he said. "Then you will be able to feel anything you want, and not have to worry about 'losing it.'"

I crumbled in relief while Ron held me. The more I cried, the closer he held me. When the tears at last subsided, I felt anger. "Try to explore the source of the anger," he advised. "In the past," I told him, "I was ignored or made fun of. After that, I learned to shut down my emotions." Organizing my experience in other ways, he suggested, would be more nourishing.

According to Ron, a therapist is someone who takes you to the door and holds your coat as you go through the doorway on your own. While going through the proverbial doorway, I could sense in my heart, rather than in my mind, that I was grieving because Mike had never been in love. I felt his desolation, as well as my own.

December 12, 1980

I want to teach women how to support themselves and one another. Sisterhood is critical to women's well-being. I would like to work in a women's group—to challenge our limiting beliefs and be challenged in return.

December 17, 1980

I am overtired and feeling guilty that I have not changed this self-destructive pattern. I work hard, then crash. Kelli-Lynne has been sick, and in a way, I am jealous of all the time she has to rest. I suspect that sickness, like overexertion, is a way of becoming passive.

Earlier in the day, Kelli-Lynne and I went Christmas shopping. Trying hard to help her enjoy our adventure, I took her to her favorite stores, but she complained that they were too crowded and didn't have anything she wanted. When I asked her what she wanted, she shot back, "How should *I* know? I'm only a *kid*." As a treat, we had supper at McDonald's, her favorite place to eat. She grumbled about the food and hardly ate at all. While we were looking over her shopping list to decide where to go next, she announced that she was bored and would shop some other time. I told her I wouldn't have any more free time before Christmas, so she'd better buy what she wanted now. She pouted.

The moment we got back to the house, she complained that she was hungry. I reminded her that we had just left McDonald's and I would not be making supper. When I put her to bed, she announced somewhat triumphantly, "I am still unhappy."

I wish I could banish pain and suffering from our lives.

January 9, 1981

I am delighted to be with a group of women for a four-day centering workshop. According to the workshop leader, there are three ways of being in the world: acquiescent, resistant, and centered. I realize that I acquiesce by being tired or confused, then I move quickly into resistance, where I protect myself with stubbornness, withdrawal, sometimes even illness. Centering is a process, not a static condition.

In my conflicts with others, I exaggerate my stubbornness by tightening up and withholding my voice and energy. Then I hide out until I feel abused. Ultimately, I protect myself by shutting down my emotions, whereupon the cycle deepens. I pay dearly for the grudges I hold.

January 12, 1981

I woke up feeling my age. As I approach thirty-seven, I am told, half my life is over. I am considered middle-aged.

I seldom spend time in front of a mirror, but this morning I noticed wrinkles around my eyes, a body that is no longer slim in all the right places, and white tufts of hair outlining my face. It all seems to have happened so suddenly. Looking closely in the mirror, I saw a reflection of clear brown eyes filled with pain and love. I have certainly let life affect me.

If feeling my age means accepting my experience, then I have more accepting to do. I am not yet in touch with the joy that must have colored earlier segments of my life. I intuit that joy is the flip side of pain, but I don't see it reflected in the mirror. The good news is that I am at last willing to see what I see, know what I know, and be who I am!

February 17, 1981

In allowing myself to be as I am, I am coming to believe less in magic and more in my own power. I wait less and ask more. How thrilling it would be conduct workshops in the same way a maestro directs an orchestra!

March 7, 1981

In last night's dream, Mike was fifteen years old, and we were taking a winter walk together along railroad tracks bordering an ice-covered pond. As we walked up a little hill, I warned him not to fool around near the ice. Glancing behind me, I suddenly saw his head above the water. I screamed and ran down the hill to pull him out, but his body was too heavy for me. As I yelled for help, I noticed a haunting smile on his face. I wondered, Does he know something about death that I don't? Strangers came, and together we dragged Mike out of the water and up the hill to a garage. But he was already dead. Then the telephone rang and woke me up.

Nowhere is there resolution, I mused, not even in my dreams. I fool myself by thinking I am over the pain of my son's death. Though I don't speak of him often, I do keep his picture in my wallet. And while searching for a credit card, I am occasionally startled by his face. I catch a breath, as if the wind has been knocked out of me, and I carry on. The thought of removing his picture from my wallet is unbearable.

Mike's death was not fair. I wonder what he would have been like now, what he would have looked like. How would he feel about *me,* about the *world?* What would his future have held? What sort of relationship would he have had with Kelli-Lynne? Most of all, I question whether we all will be together again in the future.

Women must learn to understand themselves—to be grounded in messages of their bodies, and to accept their intuitive mode of perceiving in order to lay the path for a more humane society.
　　　　　　　　—Natalie Rogers

Year Five

April 13, 1981

My heart palpitations intensified, so I made an appointment with my gynecologist. While sitting in her waiting room today, I tried to avoid looking at the pregnant bellies of the women next to me and across the room. My belly felt pregnant with grief, not a child. In retrospect I see that I had had no place to direct my anger about having a complete hysterectomy in my early thirties, so I swallowed my rage and grief. And then Mike died three months later, which generated more anger, more grief. I have been short of breath and life for the past four years!

April 21, 1981

I am beginning to understand that a woman's journey is a quest for vision, and in the process, a turning away from the familiar. Truths once taken for granted blur and disappear. Answers that previously satisfied no longer hold meaning. Relationships, too, feel empty, as old, worn-out roles are discarded.

Journeying into the unknown is always solitary. And once the descent has begun, there is no compromise. A woman's survival requires new myths and new meanings—in other words, a full-blown exercise in creativity.

My hysterectomy, for example, forced me to reassess my belief in my body's ability to support me in its customary ways. Mike's death twelve weeks later catapulted me farther into the void. The impending divorce finally pushed me into confronting my own truths. Looking back, I can see each of these events as an initiation. With each successive loss, illusions and pipe dreams became sacrificed to a greater good—namely, increased vulnerability.

Writing has helped me map this voyage. Not even with close friends did I share the shedding of definitions and the pain left behind by so much loss and internal erosion. I reserved for my journal the litanies of loneliness: my panic about how I would pay the bills addressed solely to me, my emptiness, my frustrations.

A women's group, had I known of one, might have encouraged me to fight for what I deserved, confronted me when I was feeling victimized, challenged me while I was "protecting" my friends by remaining silent, and held me accountable when I felt consumed by guilt. How eagerly I listen to women's stories of loss, dismemberment, betrayal, and passion. And the more I listen, the more confident I feel about telling my own story. From deep within my heart, I know that to name the journey is to affirm the power of the quest.

April 23, 1981

The divorce hearing is scheduled to take place in four days. I feel less angry at Gil. I had hoped to be feeling relieved, free, but instead I am sad that I have not tended the "garden" well enough.

April 24, 1981

I am at Birdsong Farm in North Berwick, attending a workshop called Music and the Soul's Journey. The timing feels perfect. My soul yearns for music and naked laughter.

I am discovering that my soul's desire is to teach women how to integrate their life and death experiences with their spirituality. The music has awakened a host of ideas and questions that seem to have been tumbling around in my mind like stones in a rock polishing machine:

I no longer want to be a "groan-up."

How am I responding to, and responsible for, my own soul's journey?

Transitions are opportunities to stop pretending.

As I surrender my compulsion to understand, I seem to know more.

I want to refrain from overextending my energy on grudges.

I have allowed myself to fall victim to what I thought was appropriate behavior.

Is it possible to become addicted to pain and deprivation?

Insight is the substitution of an old perception with a new one.

We name ourselves by the choices we make. What, then, is my name?

April 29, 1981

My divorce is at last final, and I shall begin a new life. I have no desire to celebrate, for I feel like a rag doll.

May 4, 1981

Mike would have been nineteen this day. I imagine he would be finishing his first year of college. In this fifth year of acknowledging his birthday without his physical presence, I have changed. I no longer expect family members to call, or need to retreat to the friary. I have even outgrown the need for a ritual to honor the occasion. Now I carry Mike in my heart. Remembering and loving him is enough.

July 2, 1981

Mothering a daughter is a challenge! As a mother to Mike, I relied on many of the same dynamics used with me when I was a child. I was not satisfied, and I imagine he was not, either. Parenting Kelli-Lynne is another story entirely. By thirty and a half years of age, I had become certain that I was different from my mother and that Kelli-Lynne was different from me.

July 4, 1981

*H*appy Independence Day indeed! I feel like a firecracker. Hot flashes have taken over my body and my life. No matter what I do—other than taking the estrogen pills—I cannot control their intensity or their duration. The supplements still make me cringe whenever I swallow one. Estrogen has not been around nearly as long as women have. What are *their* secrets? Where are their voices, their stories?

September 7, 1981

*T*his is Kelli-Lynne's first day of second grade. And this is the first autumn I did not calculate what grade Mike would be entering if he were alive.

In front of me are outlines I have designed for workshop proposals on time management, stress management, and assertiveness training. The irony is, I want to *write*.

September 9, 1981

*K*elli-Lynne wandered into my office and asked me what I was doing.
"Writing," I replied.
"About what?" she inquired.
"My life," I responded.
"You're always bragging about yourself," she declared.
I breathed and smiled. I had no defense; nor did I know what sparked this judgment.

September 10, 1981

*T*ime to practice time management. First, I want to write. Second, I want to do more counseling. Third, I want to shift my focus without committing to a long-term change.

September 15, 1981

*T*wo clients canceled today. Seeing their calls as an affirmation of my intention to write, I did not panic over the loss of income. Right away, I set pen to paper. Whenever I take time to write I am filled with appreciation.

September 21, 1981

I spent the afternoon sailing with friends. I succumbed fully to the capriciousness of the wind and tossing waves, all the while licking salt water from my lips. Not once did I reprimand myself for having neglected to study the "techniques" of sailing. I simply enjoyed the seafaring voyage.

October 1, 1981

Since school started, Kelli-Lynne has been talking more about Mike. Today she told me she had been imagining what he will be like when he returns. Surprised, I reminded her that he would not be residing with us again. She shook her head and told me that her father had said Mike was living in another country which, to her, meant that at some point he would be coming home. I took a breath, searching for a way to counteract this denial of death, of life, of denial itself. Rather than add to her confusion by suggesting that what her father had told her was not real, I said that I believed her brother was living in another *dimension*, and would not be returning to live with us because that doesn't happen when someone dies.

I reminded her that Mike had been dead for four years and we had not seen him. Then I patted her head, held her hand, and suggested we take a walk in the autumn leaves. As we scuffled through the dead leaves that lined the sides of the street, I pointed out to her that after a leaf falls from a tree, it dies and does not return to the branch that was once its home. Kelli-Lynne nodded and said she already knew that. We held hands and continued to wend our way through the fallen foliage, laughing at the sounds the dead leaves were making under our feet.

October 30, 1981

Someone asked me today if I was attached to suffering.

"No," I replied. "I'm attached to loving, and they seem to coexist in a way I do not yet understand." But I wonder if I am fooling myself.

October 31, 1981

A haunting event occurred at Birdsong Farm early on this Halloween Day. It all started when Nancy and I decided to take a break from the supervision group. She and I usually make time to talk about our lives, perhaps because the death of her husband coincided with that of my son.

Accompanied by Shiva, the farm dog, we had walked about a mile, and had just passed a farmhouse bearing a Beware of Dog sign when a large German shepherd dashed out in front of us. I was terrified; even Shiva was shaking. Only after someone from the farmhouse called the dog back did the muscles in my neck begin to relax.

As we continued our walk, I caught sight of something curled up in a tall bush; it looked like a small mouse. Moving closer, I noticed it had wings. I shook the underlying branch gently, but the "mouse" did not move.

Nancy, having joined me, asked, "Haven't you ever seen a bat, Rosie?"

"Only in horror movies," I replied.

"Well, after all, this *is* Halloween," she said lightly.

I gulped, trying to discharge the fear I was feeling. "Maybe this bat is some kind of omen," I whispered.

We continued our walk in silence. I did not know how to articulate my fear; besides, I imagined Nancy would accuse me of being superstitious, or perhaps silly. As we rounded a bend, I called for Shiva. When she did not respond, I wondered if my unsettled feelings were somehow associated with her. I yelled for her as loud as I could.

"What do you think has happened?" I asked Nancy.

"She's probably off being a dog," she replied with a lightness I did not share.

Heading back to the farm, we both called for Shiva repeatedly, but there was no sign of her anywhere. As we rounded the bend that led to the farmhouse with the sign, we saw a woman leaning over something on the side of the road. Walking closer, along fresh tire tracks, we saw it was the German shepherd. The dog was still breathing, but its underside had been ripped open and blood was oozing out of its stomach cavity.

"What happened?" I asked in a squeaky voice.

"He ran into the road to play with your dog and was hit by a car," the woman replied.

Looking away from the dying dog, I asked the woman if she had called a veterinarian. At that moment, out of the corner of my eye, I saw the door to the farmhouse open and a tall man carrying a shotgun climb down the front stairs. Sunlight flashed off the barrel of the gun, causing everything around us to shimmer.

∞ ∞

The woman looked at us and said quickly, "You'd better leave fast. I don't know what he might do—he loved his dog so much."

I reached out to touch her hand, to tell her I was sorry, but she pulled away and urged us again to leave immediately. We hurried off. Spotting Shiva several yards up the road, we ran to catch up with her. As we reached her, we heard one deafening shot.

My mind raced. Five minutes earlier or later and we would not have been witness to any part of this tragedy. The abruptness of the act sparked a foreboding sense that the tall man might hunt *us* down. We were, after all, the responsible party. If only we had not taken Shiva, if only we had walked in a different direction, if only the car hadn't appeared, if only . . . I was torturing myself the same way as I did when Mike was killed.

The violence disturbs me still, although six hours have passed since the dog was shot. I am once again reminded of how fragile and unpredictable life is, and of how easy it is to be in the wrong place at the wrong time.

The other therapists in our group are downstairs in costumes, celebrating Halloween. I feel too solitary to participate, too isolated, as if I am being prepared for more death. I shudder, in one of those full-body responses to truth, for I sense deep inside that more loss is imminent.

November 1, 1981

 $\mathscr{T}$ he first month of my declaration to write at least three full days a week has passed. I have written. I have taken notes. And I have realized that three days is not enough. To be conscientious, I would need to devote two months to writing full-time.

When I returned to my office today, I found a message from my mother stating that my grandfather was hospitalized with pneumonia. She called this turn of events the "old man's blessing," reminding me that my father's father was relieved of his misery when he died of pneumonia.

I canceled my afternoon appointments and drove straight to the hospital. My grandfather's bed was empty when I arrived. I panicked, imagining that he had died before I'd had a chance to say good-bye. The patient in the next bed assured me that Bomp had gone for X rays.

One hour passed. I kept sentinel outside his room, pacing the corridors and memorizing the names on every door. Another hour passed. I fidgeted, plagued with questions. Why keep a sick man in the X-ray unit for two hours? A nurse assured me he would be returning to his room within ten minutes.

I was there when he was wheeled into his room. As soon as he was comfortably settled, I sat next to his bed and held his hand tightly.

"Hi, Bomp," I said lightly. I knew he was not doing well.

The moment the nurse left, he introduced me to his roommate. "This is my granddaughter who teaches at the university and writes books and does retreats and . . ."

I stayed quietly by his side, feeling his love for me. As usual, I was embarrassed but also appreciative of the pride he took in my life. When he finished, I told him how much I loved him. He stared at me intently, as if memorizing my face. He asked about Kelli-Lynne, and I assured him she was fine and would send him a healing picture. When he began talking about going fishing with Mike, I knew he was dying. It was as though the two of us had a secret code. I leaned over and told him that I knew he and Mike would have a wonderful reunion. Our tears merged, then ran down his face. His eyes closed.

"Not yet, Bomp!" I wanted to scream. "You can't die yet." But instead of saying a word, I took his thin hands in mine. He turned his head and opened his eyes a little.

"June, is that you?"

Squeezing his hands, I again lowered my face to his, and said softly, "I love you."

I knew I was standing in for my mother, saying the words he had for decades longed to hear her say. His eyes closed, and a faint smile flickered across his pale lips. Everything before me blurred.

A nurse appeared and told me he needed to rest. So I kissed him gently, headed for the parking lot, and drove home.

November 2, 1981

*M*y mother called in the middle of the night to tell me my grandfather had died. My first thought upon hanging up the phone was that I had lost an ally. I felt sad for me, yet relieved for him. His battle was over.

Granted, my grandfather was demanding and at times an emotional tyrant, but he was *real*—you never had to guess what he was feeling or thinking. Seldom did he bow to obligations or attend Christmas gatherings, weddings, or funerals. He was selfish at times and expected the family to adjust.

I smiled in appreciation as I remembered the birthday party we had "delivered" to him in September. Even then, I knew it would be the last time Kelli-Lynne and I would celebrate his birthday with him. Lovingly, we had prepared a feast, blown up balloons, and sat down to party with him. My grandmother—his wife of sixty-three years—brought out the cake while I surprised him with the last rose of summer, which I had picked from my garden.

When Kelli-Lynne woke up in the morning, I told her Bomp had died. She asked if he was with Mike now. I said I didn't know, but she stopped me short, explaining that she knew they were together. Then she suggested that we send healing energy to Bomp. We held hands; took deep, long breaths; and showered him with white, healing light. His energy felt solid and steady—so different from Mike's, shortly after he died.

"Yup, he is with Mike, Mom. Don't worry," she said with authority.

After a while we set off for my grandmother's house. Arriving at her front door, I looked up at the window where Bomp's face had greeted me for the past thirty-four years. Kelli-Lynne squeezed my hand and said, "Bomp doesn't need a window to see us now, Mom." How did she know what I was thinking?

Nanny sat in her kitchen looking lost. I worked my way past several family members, sat beside her, and reached for her hand. Every time she started to cry, someone told her she had to pull herself together and be strong. I was appalled. The messages sounded painfully familiar. This time, however, I was able to see through to the core of the anguish: the greatest family fear is that if anyone shows emotion, others might be forced to face *their* feelings. Where, I wondered, is the softness? Where are the hugs? Whre is the family hysteric?

I wanted to comfort my grandmother, for she looked so small and young. I patted her hand and assured her that it was okay to cry, because she was sad. Then *I* cried. Kelli-Lynne came up to us and asked why other people were not crying. Even more saddened, I cried harder.

Why should a woman act composed after being abandoned by the man she shared her life with for more than six decades? Why should she be expected to make it easy for us? Sure, I had performed admirably right after Mike's death, only to crumble into depression afterward. No one has the right to tell Nanny to be quiet! I don't think it is possible to express emotions with dignity.

December 17, 1981

*N*anny spent the past four days here. She has aged considerably since Bomp's death. "I'm just an old lady," she repeated more times than I can remember, and kept asking me what I wanted from her apartment so she could write it into her will. "I don't know how long I will live," she reiterated, as if hoping that death would take *her* as well. The only time I sensed her energy was when she complained about "those social security people." Her anger reminds her that she is alive.

I wonder if we could have done something to prepare her for Bomp's death. She goes through the motions of talking and eating and caring for herself, and all the while she knows she is not feeling. She leans on me when she walks. How easily I could take over her life, yet I do not want to dishonor her by infantilizing her.

My mother assumes that Nanny will throw herself into church work. "That's what widows do," she told me.

"Why in hell should she throw herself into *anything?*" I asked.

"To be busy," my mother said without emotion.

"Life is more than being busy," I retorted sharply. "She won't forget by being busy. She has to feel, grieve, recover her own meaning." I was secretly impressed with the passion of my knowing.

Christmas 1981

*T*he only gift Nanny requested for Christmas was peace of mind. At dinner I proposed a toast to the lives and memories of Mike and Bomp.

January 4, 1982

*S*now is falling in large, heavy wet flakes. I warm my bare legs by the fire, music playing in the background. My heart feels warmed, too. What realizations, dreams, relationships, and deaths will manifest in the new year?

I have been struck by a sense of my ordinariness since Nanny's visit. In particular, I recognize how severely I blind myself to my own cycles of change and growth when I look to others for help. Last night I conducted a futile search for a book to fill me with insight or hope. Paging through six volumes, I found nothing, yet the quest kept me busy. All the while, I watched myself with amusement, thinking, "There she goes again, looking beyond herself for understanding and meaning."

January 6, 1982

*W*ill my writing be forever postponed to a time when there are no dishes or clothes to wash, no child to care for, no telephone to answer? For two decades I have grounded myself by setting pen to paper, yet I have not taken my urge to write seriously. When I am not distracted by others, I find ways to distract myself. At times I fantasize existing in a state of nonattachment to people and places, sensing all. Other times I am pained by seeing and knowing too much.

January 21, 1982

I have found my rhythm, at least for this week. I see clients one day and write the following day. Today, I surprised myself by surrendering to a midday nap. I am becoming flexible enough to guiltlessly let go of old ways of doing things, especially those that do not honor my inclinations.

January 24, 1982

*I*n a dream I had last night, I arrived at a large building fronted by many high windows. As I walked through the doorway into a spacious open area, a man greeted me and announced that the family would soon be coming. I reacted with a jolt. I had no idea what I was doing there.

The "family" arrived, and I began observing a counseling session between a forty-year-old aunt and her twelve-year-old nephew. The therapist said, "Pretend I am not here, and relate as you normally do."

The boy addressed his aunt sarcastically. She shrugged and ignored his comments. He continued to try to provoke her while she continued to pretend that everything was okay.

"What usually happens now?" inquired the therapist.

The boy walked over and began punching and kicking his aunt. She refused to defend herself. The therapist intervened and wrestled with the boy, quickly defeating him. The aunt remained outwardly calm.

I was fascinated by the boy. Intuitively I knew that he wanted to be touched, that his acting out was a plea for attention and love. I approached him cautiously. He responded by curling into a tight ball. Holding his arms, I helped him curl up even more tightly. I asked him what he needed in order to be more comfortable. He maintained his silence. Then I put my hands over his eyes, whereupon he began to sob. Covering him with my body, I began to hum and rock him, asking nothing of him.

Only then was I aware that both the aunt and the therapist were watching me. For about ten seconds I felt self-conscious. Finally the therapist said to me, "That was one of the most magnificent sessions I have ever witnessed. How did you know what to do?"

"I listened to my intuition and followed its energy so it could complete itself," I said sincerely.

Upon awakening, I realized that my words to the therapist signify how I wish to work and how I intend to live my life.

February 24, 1982

In supervision group I announced that I was proud of my commitment to write. For the first time, I was unafraid of affirming myself publicly. Perhaps affirmations of this sort are what cause my seven-year-old daughter to repeat the family adage "Don't brag." Over the past five years my feelings of competence have inspired guilt. What right do I have to feel proud or to be successful when my son is dead? What will people think? Over and over again I have stalemated myself by recalling that I am the mother of a dead son. No longer do I want to validate Mike's existence by denying my own happiness. I refuse to dedicate myself to a life of mediocrity!

Last year was the year of coping. This is the year of competence.

March 3, 1982

I am thirty-eight years old on this day. Determined to begin my birthday by writing, I sat down at the typewriter, and the following words appeared in front of me:

Yes, dear one, quietness lifts your spirits while life is weighing upon you. Take time each day to listen to your breathing, to music, and to your own voice, which echoes eternity.

March 12, 1982

I am discovering new ways of connecting. Writing is one of them. Expressing my feelings verbally is another. Insisting on honesty is a third. Most of all, I am learning that a woman's way is mysterious, circuitous, intuitive, creative, receptive, and punctuated with pauses and interruptions. A woman's way is a tapestry that spirals, filled with temptations to wait, to accommodate, to care for the world. A woman's way is triumphant, eventually.

I want to be allied with the events of my daily life.

March 15, 1982

Yesterday, during a family systems workshop, I was asked to play the role of a woman guided by the aphorism "See no evil, hear no evil, speak no evil." What little power resides in being "nice"!

Today, I was invited to play a grandmother whose infant grandson was killed. Broken-hearted as a result of my grandson's death, I clung to my daughter. I blamed us both for his death, and felt empowered by my accusations. I wanted to scream at her, "If only you had let me bring him up, he would be alive now." As the bereaved grandmother, I decided never to be close to anyone again.

On the drive home I wondered if my mother and her mother had blamed me for Mike's death. Just as I was beginning to search my mind for clues, I was stopped by a police officer because I did not have my headlights on.

March 18, 1982

Spring fever. I perch with bare legs on the back porch. My shirt sleeves are rolled up, inviting the sun to tan my skin and to heal the red, itchy bumps that have appeared on my arms. Yesterday I renounced my boots; today I am mentally directing the snow to melt so I can touch the earth with my bare feet. Spring is the season in which I feel most childlike. It is also when I miss Mike the most.

While drinking in the sunlight, I remember that each spring Mike and I would conspire to find the perfect maple trees to sap. Our bounty of

∞ ∞

carefully chosen trees was always kept secret, lest other kids attempt to pirate them. We'd trudge through the snow-carpeted woods without saying a word. Selecting the first tree was always a ritual. Upon finding a promising candidate, we would crane our necks to see how close to the sky it reached, then we would measure its girth by encircling it with our arms, pause, and hug it to express our gratitude. Sometimes we even smacked our lips, as if tasting the fully boiled maple syrup. Walking home, we would whisper about the design of the season's plugs and reminisce about the many years we had sapped together.

Once home, Mike would draw an elaborate map showing the location of the trees, and together we would design the plugs. For me, the acts of plugging the trees, checking the pails daily, gathering the sap, and even boiling it down lacked the excitement sparked by our initial foray into the woods. When the weather became warm enough, we would return to the trees we had plugged, bow to each one, and leave the woods until the next sapping season.

These days, I do not sap. I do, however, surround myself with flowers during the entire month of March to honor my birthday and the day Mike died. I still examine trees with a sapper's eye, and I allow memories of eight years amid the trees to connect me with Mike.

I watch the calendar as March 23 creeps up. I know from experience that I will live through the day. As before, I want the pain of missing Mike to go away, but I no longer try, or even hope, to "make sense of" his death. I live my life honestly, with as much integrity as is possible considering the many truths that coexist within me.

Consistency is no longer relevant, for life itself is inconsistent. I am aware that the truth I value today may change by tomorrow, or next month, or next year. Meanwhile, I wait in silence, trusting that as I develop the courage to speak my truth, I will become my truth . . . until another one takes it place. And I write, for the sake of continuity—which is altogether different from consistency.

March 22, 1982

*K*elli-Lynne is sick. She knows that tomorrow is another anniversary of Mike's death. Sickness and sadness seem to merge for her. They do for me, as well.

March 23, 1982

The fifth anniversary of Mike's death. I opened my eyes to a sunny day, not the steely gray one of five years past. After breakfast, I arranged for a babysitter and went to my supervision group as planned. Soon after I arrived, one of the women said she would like to see a picture of my son, so I passed around the photo of him that I keep in my wallet.

The group urged me to talk about Mike. I began by sharing the sense of isolation I felt while giving birth to him, the pain of being unprepared for motherhood, my subsequent divorce from his father, and the hardship of attending college while being solely responsible for a young child. I explained that I had always felt more like Mike's older sister than his mother, and went on to describe some of the struggles we had survived as he careened into his teenage years. Everyone listened, and nobody judged me. In this atmosphere of unconditional acceptance, I let loose the pain and loneliness I had been holding for so many years. Between sobs, I assured everyone that I had done the best I could. Then I repeated the promise I had made when Mike was one month old, I was eighteen, and his father had just walked out on us: I would take care of him no matter what.

One of the women moved closer and asked me to hold her tightly and "make noises" into her shoulder. Immediately my body began to tremble, then I caved into her and wailed. Catching my breath, I stammered, "I'm s-sorry, Mike. I did the b-best I could."

Another woman asked me to share what I enjoyed most about Mike. I described the times we spent sapping trees, and mentioned how much I appreciated his wit, his intellectual curiosity, his risk-taking attitude, and his love for the woods and the ocean.

"The truth is," I said, "that I did not know how to love when Mike was a child." Sobbing once more, I let myself feel the tragedy of my words and my lack of experience. "I deeply regret that we were not able to grow into love together," I explained. "I know all about broken hearts now."

Moments later I could see with absolute clarity that I was a different person than I had been while Mike was growing up. And I realized that although I had convinced myself to the contrary, I had not finished punishing myself for his death. I returned home feeling worn out and somehow integrated.

The conscious feminine
is forever forgiving.
    —Brooke Alexander

Year Six

April 13, 1982

I had a miniature class reunion with four women I was close to in college sixteen years ago. Before seeing them, I was afraid they had not heard about Mike's death, and I did not want to tell the story all over again. I also worried that we would have only the past in common. As it turned out, they all knew about Mike's death, and we had a number of shared experiences.

After reminiscing, we summarized all the "nevers" that had become part of our lives. The more we talked, the clearer it became that although we were all explorers in a sense, we were each at a different stage of discovery. I do not envy any of these women. I would take my present and my past over anyone else's.

As a result of this evening's reunion, I have a yearning to understand what the feminine journey is all about. I want to invite other women to join me in comparing voyages, myths, and especially initiations.

May 4, 1982

If Mike had lived, he would be twenty years old today. He has been dead for five years; my grandfather has been dead for six months. *Dead* is a stagnant word that goes nowhere.

Determined to negate this state of "no movement," I sit by the ocean to write a birthday letter to Mike.

Happy birthday, Mike:

I was your birther. Your birth and your death continue to have a great impact on my life. I take time out today to sit by the water and write to you. Sailboats dot the horizon, clouds adorn the blue sky, a seagull glides by in search of food.

I don't know how to stop celebrating your birthday. Kelli-Lynne used to bake cakes for you even when she knew you could not eat them. I watch the seagull pecking vehemently through a bag of trash and realize that I, too, feel like a scavenger searching for morsels of life's food.

Mike, I try to imagine you as a separate spirit, but I feel my link to you as a mother. Intellectually, I understand that our bond as mother and son existed only in this physical world, but I don't know how to define you now. In truth, I never knew how to define you. Many of our conflicts resulted from my thwarted attempts to somehow characterize you.

A few weeks ago, I became aware that I have been keeping myself from feeling successful, competent, and happy. I allow myself to take in only enough air to fill my lungs. I don't fill my heart. I know this sounds weird, but I have connected your death with my pain even while recalling the happy, silly times we shared. I have been honoring your memory by cutting off my own vitality. Starting today, I will honor us both in a more life-enhancing way: I will speak, walk, dance, play, and be who I am.

I will miss not having you in my world. Yet, missing you will no longer choke me or lead me away from my potential. I want for myself what I always wanted for you: love, laughter, intimacy, spontaneity, creativity, and appreciation for life.

I do love you. I love you with a greater depth now, five years after your death, than I was capable of during your lifetime. As I grow and let my heart absorb more of life, I imagine I will love you more. For now, the greatest gift I can extend to you is to honor who I am becoming.

There are no good-byes. I greet you once again, and end this letter with hugs.

Love,

Mom

As soon as I finish, a poem fills the rest of the page.

I honor you on this day of your birth, my son,
By the sea where, as I celebrate
Your birthing and your dying,
I celebrate, also, my emergence.

I honor you by loving myself,
By forgiving myself
For being only human, after all.

I honor you with flowers in my home.
I honor you by residing in quietness,
Beside the ocean that has always been your home.

Here we scattered the ashes of your life.
And I continue to imagine your spirit moving wherever water flows.
I honor you each time I see water.
I honor you by claiming my soul.

May 5, 1982

I am exhausted from a dream I had last night. I was a guest at a huge house owned by a real estate broker. Other guests were touring the rooms and, like me, were impressed with their high, spacious walls and white ceilings. I knew without being told that I had been invited because someone had died and I was to help people grieve. I didn't recognize the adults here, though I did know the children. Walking into a room, I comforted a teenager as she cried. I held her and assured her that crying was okay.

In the next scene, Mike and I were in the wilderness, climbing over rocks high above a waterfall. He was leading the way, and was much farther up the rocks than I was. I asked him to be careful, then told him to come down to a less dangerous elevation. He took one step, slipped, and tumbled into the waterfall. As I watched in horror, his body crashed into sharp rocks, turning and rolling with the currents, and I could not get to the bottom in time to help him.

I raced to the house and screamed for help. Someone suggested calling the warden's office, but as it turned out, the warden could not come for twenty-four hours because he was "all booked up." So I asked for high rubber boots and a microphone, thinking that if Mike heard my voice, he would be less afraid. Someone handed me a pair of boots and a megaphone.

As I set off, a woman reminded me that I could not leave because I had a commitment to student teaching and this was the day she had decided to give me my own class. She adamantly demanded that I find someone to cover the class before going to Mike. To hell with teaching, I told myself, I have to let Mike know I am here for him.

I left, and others followed behind me. Searching in the growing darkness, I yelled Mike's name through the megaphone, but there was no answer. How I wished I had an instrument capable of picking up his voice! I made my way through the bushes that covered the water. Still no sign of him. The sun had dropped well below the horizon, yet I refused to give up.

While other people left, I searched on. Then I said aloud, "Rosie, stop putting yourself through all this, because even if you do find him alive in the dream, he is really dead. What's the point of this hell you are creating for yourself?" Then I woke up.

As I reflect on the dream message, I see myself trying to connect with Mike in the everyday world of experience. The truth is, of course, that my connection to Mike bridges dimensions and I do not serve the bonds we share by attempting to reach him through ordinary channels. When we are "speaking" together, megaphones are not needed. And I must trust this intangible reality even when I am with those who are more concerned with student teaching and other external responsibilities. I am being taught by spirit.

May 7, 1982

*G*rief and creativity are parts of every woman's experience. We all love and lose, let go and leave, give birth and release our newborns to the world. We all grow up grieving.

Creativity, on the other hand, is more elusive. What is a creative lifestyle? How can we as women learn to accept and embrace the grief inherent in a creative lifestyle? These are the questions I have been asking myself lately.

At times, I am tempted to enroll in a postgraduate program and become "degreed" again. More often, I know that life is my postdoctoral curriculum, my truest source of wisdom. I speak the language of experience to express the unfolding of my soul. Where are the teachers of "soul sense"?

June 20, 1982

*D*oes a sorcerer hold the resources? Is a sorcerer the same as a wizard?

I have been dreaming about sorcerers and wizards. How I long to reside in the consciousness extolled by Henry David Thoreau, when he wrote, "Our truest life is when we are in our dreams, awake."

My dreams highlight choices and changes. Trust, I am finding, is a prerequisite to entering both grief and the creative process. I am also discovering that a midlife crisis is brought on by events, not age, and that I've been immersed in a midlife crisis since the age of thirty-three.

June 28, 1982

*T*his past week I again taught at CPSI. For the first time, I worked with small groups of people rather than the usual class of six hundred. My interactions were imbued with integrity, perhaps because I at last refused to succumb to the myth that one should always be happy, open, and creative. Sometimes I was tired; other times I missed Kelli-Lynne. I displayed both my fatigue and my sadness.

A friend at the institute had a vision of Mike's energy. She saw a brilliant light illuminating the entire room and received this message from him: "Tell my mother I love her very much." When my friend described her experience, I cried. Without saying a word, I wandered off to the planetarium where, surrounded by darkness and Zen music, I felt nothing but love. My tears were not laden with sadness or pain; they were tears of pure expression.

Teaching myths and rituals plunged me into a sea of archetypes. I surfaced with an enhanced understanding of why I'm drawn toward working with women: our initiations and journeys, our dances and celebrations, and our ways of knowing are not only intertwined but connected to the universe itself.

July 3, 1982

For the past two days, the energy in my hands and forehead has been pulsating. My hands feel like they are on fire, and my forehead hurts. Picking up a pencil this evening, I began to wonder if what people refer to as automatic writing is the same phenomenon as the "blink-truths" that have been appearing in my journal since Mike's death.

Before I had a chance to ponder this question further, the following message showed up on the page in front of me.

From dusk to dawn, I come to guide you between the two realms. I blanket you in sleep, dense like the fog, waiting. Gently, ever so gently, I lift you from your familiar world and take you back to your true beginnings, that which you know of as home.

Gently, I imbue you with wisdom, careful not to disturb you or give you reason to fear. And I smile softly as you wonder about the source of the guidance.

You have much to learn and much to teach. When you give of yourself, you are truly giving from the source. You are now firmly connected with the source of all. Use candles and flowers to steady your gaze. Look deeply within the peach rose. Smell of the essence. Notice how each petal ripples into the next; how all petals are connected to form the rose. So, too, are you formed— layer upon layer, year upon year, dream upon dream.

July 4, 1982

I enjoy the surprise of picking up my pen and inviting guidance. The words seem to affect me even before they are recorded on the page.

Believe in yourself. We are here. Rejoice in your body. Calmness pervades spirit. Remember your beginnings, for they hold the sparks of divine intelligence. Stay with the light. Truly, we are here. Create a space and time for us to speak through you. Then we will all majestic be. Cease the chaos that envelops you. Be still. Begin to guide your work with our voices. We await your invitation.

Concentrate on the light, for we are all from one light source. We are all aspects of the divine inspiration you have been drawing near to you. Blessed be the spirit, and blessed be the body. All is one in the light. Always remember, divinity resides within. The sounds of our voices exist in eternity.

Every word resonates with all that has ever been spoken. No thoughts are ever lost.

Bodies are only a manifestation in your earthly dimension. We are the light within you and all beings and all things. The flame of life is living within you. Sing praises each day. Bow to the trees and know that they, too, share life with you. Ask not advice about cosmic matters from mortals; they know not. Ask of the light. Ask of the stars. Ask of the sun and moon.

The path of rejoicing is the natural way of the unencumbered soul. Pain, struggle, suffering, and endings are detours. The absence of joy is akin to "endings," and there are no endings, only joylessness. Grace and joy perpetuate light.

Healing encompasses grace. Suffering is a human experience. Not on this side is suffering glorified. Souls manifest in purity, both here and in your dimension. Growth does not derive from pain.

Straying from the light creates pain and isolation. You incarnated to activate your soul to receive and express grace in human ways. The ways of grace are individual and connected to each person's unique soul purpose.

July 7, 1982

Before writing in my journal this afternoon, I decided to pick a few beautiful red roses from the bushes in front of the house. I put them in a vase on the desk in front of me, set a candle beside them, then sat down and invited the "guides" to add their impressions to my consciousness.

Trust in the inner light reflected by the candle in front of you. Seek silence and inspiration in the roses. Invite the fragrance to envelop your soul, for roses are of the soul—a living metaphor for the beauty within. Drink of their scent. Touch their petals and you caress infinity. Overlook not the thorns, for they protect the flower. Meditate on the beauty of the rose and you draw closer to your own source.

Many are the paths which lead to me. Yet, only your path is your way. Nobody else's path will enable you to be with the light. You are responsible for detecting the one you have agreed to create for your soul. A magnetic resonance accompanies the decision to be in alignment with your soul's service.

People your life with those you love, for love is of the light. Sharing with others enables all to seek greater depths through community, but the journey itself is solitary.

Many are those who are now, as ever, serving as beacons of light to others, illuminating yet refusing to dictate.

I am amazed by the poignancy of these words, and by these guides who seem to see me and know of the candle and roses in front of me. It is as though all is transparent, even me!

July 8, 1982

Last night I dreamed I heard noises coming from the basement. Checking out the source of the sounds, I came upon two men waiting for me at the bottom of the stairs. Surprised, I asked them how long they had been there. One replied that he had been around ever since he removed the cable about a year and a half before. As he spoke, I could see he carried the same energy as Mike. He said he had been assigned to link "three levels" through the cable.

I woke up this morning thinking I was ready to begin something. What it is I do not know.

July 9, 1982

Another night, another dream. This time I was in college, with two courses to go before graduation. A class I wanted to take was filled, so the registrar tried to persuade me to sign up for another. "I'm not interested," I told him, whereupon he counted my credits and discovered I had enough to graduate.

"I'm not ready," I insisted, still hoping to take more courses. I was terrified to be cast out of school, for I knew my real work would be starting.

July 17, 1982

"Mom, how many times do you think I have been born?" asked Kelli-Lynne.

"I'm not sure," I replied.

"Well, what I mean is, how many past lives do you think I've had?"

"I don't know."

"Do you feel weird talking about past lives with people?" she asked.

"Do you feel weird talking about them to me?" I asked.

"No."

"I'm glad," I said. "Not everyone believes in past lives."

"I know I lived in 1842."

"I believe you have lived before," I told her.

"So do I." She breathed a smile of relief.

"Probably many times. And I believe you when you say you were an American Indian a couple of times."

"You weren't always a mother, you know," she explained.

"I know. But I'm glad we chose each other in this life."

"Me, too," she said, hugging me.

July 18, 1982

I am "taking dictation" again. I love the surprising blink-truths that flow effortlessly from my pen.

Draw close to your own wellsprings and you move closer to your own source, which is connected to the source. Celebrate yourself with arms outstretched.

The light you see reflected by the stars is the light within you. Become as a magnet to your own experience. Pursue your intuition with zeal. Listen for the wisdom of insight, which exists beyond words. Be prepared to leap with lightning speed, to intercept and complete translations in metaphor.

Commit yourself to expressing that which clouds your soul, for the natural condition of the soul is pure light. Anger, too, has a purity if it is experienced in its fullness and released. A clearing and a cleansing accompany the release of emotions, which add to your experience of the soul. The unnatural holding in of emotional expression creates a dimming of your natural light, and results in karma. Vibrate with your emotions. Pulsate with your own expression.

The path you have chosen to refine and purify is connected to the life experiences you will create and attract. And the emotions that induce you to be silent are aligned with that which you must regain mastery of. Allow your emotions to swell like a wave, and to crest and splash to shore ... and fear not the prospect of being beached or drowned.

July 24, 1982

Be still. *Be* even stiller. *Find* in the depths of your being that which you already know, for in this moment you know all you need to. *Living* is an opportunity to rediscover and reclaim that which has always been yours. *Meditate* on the words, "I know, I know, I know." *Repeat* this phrase several times. *Be* aware of the many ways of saying it, and recognize the understanding that comes with each intonation. *One* learns the same lessons over and over until the most minute incident serves as a reminder of what one knows to be true.

Coincidences are physical materializations in the human dimension. *Coincidences* represent the most poignant linkages for human beings, whereas in the dimension beyond, they are unknown.

The marriage of experience and knowledge brings forth wisdom. *And* people of the world are not comfortable with wisdom. *Hence,* precisely at the moment when you are drinking from your wellspring of truth, which reflects the awakening of your own love-wisdom, you circumvent the wisdom of your essence and attribute your truth to coincidence. *Your* schooling on earth is fraught with circuitous seductions, and evermost present is the temptation to betray your own truth, which is your light.

This is all so right, so profound. I read the words through tear-filled eyes. I feel so well connected and reinforced with clarity.

August 19, 1982

Quiet be. *Be* quiet. *For* in the quietness, we can connect. *Let* go of the thought-jam. *Permit* yourself to feel fully the presence of love. *Breathe* in love, and breathe out discord. *Fill* the room with love, and when you have done this, concentrate on inviting the vibrations of love to fill every pore of your body. *Experience* loving yourself. *Experience* loving others. *Surround* each thought-distraction with loving energy, and wait in quietness. *Lovingly* create more quietness inside and outside yourself. *Know* that we are forever present in the loving space.

Know that you are a channel. *Know,* too, that your ability to receive is infinite. *Moreover,* know that your purpose is to heal.

I retreat to read each line with care. The writing is loaded with levels of meaning. The next step—my real challenge—is to synthesize the information and live the principles.

August 26, 1982

I prepare to write, emptying my mind of all thoughts so I can be more receptive. The energies feel different to me this time. Or am I the one who is different? Dismissing even these questions, I concentrate on inviting the presence of the guides.

I am here, and I have been here. It is necessary for you to drop your many distractions. I watch you with love and humor.

"I am relieved you are here," I reply, "but puzzled by what you just dictated. Please explain."

Insight and clarity await you, but first you must discipline yourself. Fear results from the memories held in your emotional body. Fasting and being more particular about what you eat will gradually erase the fear. Excitement, too, will come gradually. Too much excitement is not the way to conserve energy; being in the flow produces the glow. A relaxed excitement awaits you.

"Whoa! I am trying to understand all of what you are saying, so I need you to slow down."

Calm yourself. It is not necessary to understand all at once. Allowing yourself to open is a first step. Be with courage. Permit yourself to feel good about being present rather than berating yourself for not understanding.

I work with souls who have no consciousness of dying. Some have no consciousness of living in your dimension. I help restore their memories of life and death. I try to reactivate their original allegiance to light. I chose this occupation in order to be of service.

"What does this have to do with *me?* I am alive. I was thinking you were going to say you had worked with my son, Mike."

No, I did not. He was confused initially, but he quickly let go of his earthly reality. I am here for you because you serve people who are struggling with their own essences. You will have much more to discover about grieving and loving and creating—not one of which exists without the others. I see you have many questions, so I will stop.

My head wants answers, and this search for comprehension tires me. I set down my pen and read what I have written, uncertain of where this writing has come from. With a resoluteness that surprises me, I decide to relax, trusting that this will all make sense in time.

September 10, 1982

The last few days have been timeless—no schedules, no telephone, no agendas. I painted today, then I exercised and meditated. After my mid-day meditation, I felt so relaxed that I slept for an hour. I woke up feeling wonderful.

An hour a day of exercise followed by meditation is becoming routine. Discipline used to remind me of a stern father demanding rigidity in return. Now it enables me to create a structure within which I can refine my art. I am less preoccupied with the day-to-day dramas.

September 26, 1982

I spoke to Nanny twice over the weekend. Today would have been Bomp's birthday. Last year, we brought him a birthday party; this year, I wired flowers to Nanny. I did for her what I wished someone had done for me on Mike's birthdays.

October 10, 1982

I've had a series of dreams instructing me in the meaning of light. People in my dreams teach me how to access and retain my own light. They remind me that each of us embodies an individualized expression of light from the source. I wake up knowing that these dreams offer important teachings, and that I have worked hard—and have been worked on hard—during the night.

October 20, 1982

Last weekend I walked on the beach alone, deliberately choosing to see, listen, feel, and *not write*. The tide was coming in, and the sounds of the waves breaking on the rocks mesmerized me. Pushing all thoughts aside, I concentrated on listening. I strained my ears to hear the laughing sounds the rocks made as the water drained from them and returned to the ocean. I giggled at my resentment of the waves' "intrusions" that prevented me from hearing the rocks. How unfamiliar it is to appreciate a scenario without directing the action!

November 18, 1982

I grieve the distance that has been separating me from my soul. The flow has halted, most likely because I have stopped meditating and exercising. Once again, I have to learn the lesson. When I consciously focus my energies, I am aware of light; when I retract my energies, I am aware of darkness. My intention makes all the difference.

January 11, 1983

I arranged to spend last night with my grandmother. I hadn't slept at her house since I was a little girl. We'd talked on the telephone a few times a week, sharing the outlines of our lives, but I wanted to tell her face-to-face that I loved her.

I called ahead to invite Nanny out to supper, and stopped off to buy her a bouquet of flowers. When I got to her apartment, the smell of chicken stewing on the gas stove filled my nostrils, and I wondered if she had forgotten that we were going out.

"I thought you might be too tired, or it might be too foggy tonight, so I put this together, just in case," she said.

I sighed. For years she had taken care of me, and neither one of us knew how to begin changing the old roles. I have money now, enough to treat my grandmother to supper; she has little extra money. I insisted that we go out, and she smiled. We descended the long cement steps hand in hand. I liked having her lean on me.

Over our meal, my grandmother confided her difficulties in getting used to another doctor. Three of her family doctors had died, and she didn't trust the young bearded physician who "inherited" her. Her eyes filling with tears, she said softly, "It doesn't get any easier. Everyone keeps telling me it will, but it doesn't."

I reached for her hand. I knew she was talking about living alone, without her longtime husband. I let myself be touched by her pain and by my love for her. She shifted her position, withdrew her hand, and said triumphantly, "Your grandfather would turn over in his grave if he knew his veteran's pension stopped when he died."

When our check arrived, Nanny refused the senior citizen's discount and offered to pay her half of the bill. How proud she is! I took the check, reminding her that supper was my treat.

Driving back to Nanny's house, I reflected on how different our lives are. She asked me if I was still committed to finishing my doctorate. I explained that I had stopped working on it because I couldn't do it my way. She said nothing, but I could tell she felt let down. I wanted her disappointment to go away, I wanted her to understand my decision— but alas, credentials are important to her.

Back at her apartment, Nanny glanced at the calendar and said, "My grandmother has been dead fifty-six years today." I marveled silently at her memory. More of her friends are dead than alive. All her children are alive; one great-grandchild is dead. She lives, and so do I. We are each other's heritage.

I offered her a back rub. She declined. Hesitantly, I asked how she was doing with money and reminded her that she was welcome to anything I had whenever she needed it. She looked away quickly so I wouldn't witness the trembling in her lower lip. Then she stared at the weathered, ten-year-old canvas bag I had brought my clothes in and commented on its "tackiness." I shrugged. She disappeared and returned with a new brown leather travel bag, a gift from a son far away.

"I'll never use it," she said.

Once again, she gives to me.

I slept alone in my grandmother's bed surrounded by atomizer bottles, the perfumes long dried up. Pictures of three generations of family encircled me. On one wall were pictures of me performing, all taken during the eight years I studied at dancing school. For more than thirty years the color portraits of me in motion have enveloped my grandmother at night and in the morning! History prevails.

I awakened to the world my grandmother sees each day, bordered by her thirty-inch window. I want always to remember this moment, though I don't know why. Kelli-Lynne will be sleeping in this bed next weekend. I imagine that years from now, she will tell her grandchildren about the night she slept in her great-grandmother's bed, and she, too, will count the years that elapsed since the death of her oldest known ancestor.

"Rosie, breakfast is ready," Nanny called. When I was a kid, she used to spoil me with her crispy-brown French toast, and cambric coffee Bomp had prepared especially for me. Now my grandmother was welcoming me to her table again, and was setting before me a plate of French toast. I cried.

January 15, 1983

This morning, Kelli-Lynne and I were talking like pals, rather than mother and daughter. I said, "I hope we will always be friends."

"Of course," she replied.

I want a clear, uninterrupted, honest relationship with Kelli-Lynne.

March 2, 1983

In last night's dream, I was performing in a play and was afraid I would forget my lines. Why is play such hard work? I wondered, asking to see a copy of the script. Someone handed me a copy of the story, but not the play. I already knew the story; what I needed to review were my lines. I was concerned that if I didn't have the wording right, I might throw everyone else off—in which case even the backstage prompter wouldn't know how to help us. Finally, someone handed me the script, and I was relieved to discover that I knew my lines after all.

When it was almost time for me to appear on stage, I nervously peeked through the curtain to see the audience. It was a full house, but the seats were all facing away from the stage! Still, the play went on as if everything were normal. As the dream ended, I was awaiting the reviews.

Is it possible to be "prompted" from other dimensions? I desire to lead my life without worrying about what my lines should be, and at the same time I want control over the outcome.

March 23, 1983

The day does not immobilize me. It is the day Mike died, that's all. That's enough. I chose to live the experiences of the past few days without writing, trusting that I would not lose track of myself.

All of creation is a symphony
of joy and jubilation.
　　　—Hildegarde of Bingen

Year Seven

I am en route to Spring Lake, North Carolina, for an intensive six-day workshop. As the plane slowly climbs, I hear my inner voice say, "I am on my way." I lean back and watch the receding landscape covered in places by flimsy, fast-moving clouds. It's a relief to be up in the air catching sight of the earth and knowing she remains solid. I would not choose to live in the clouds, though I do like to visit them.

April 12, 1983

Part of the advanced training at the workshop was a seance. The leader, Patricia, asked us to invite to the session someone who had been dead for no more than five years. Because Mike has been dead for six years, I figured he was not a candidate. Then Patricia surprised me by asking why I hadn't volunteered my son.

"It's been too long," I said simply.

"Rosie, the staff has reason to believe that your son is trying to communicate with you. If you agree, we would like to invite him to the seance. But you'll want to know that others will be present, including a television crew that will be filming the event, as well as Dr. William Roll, a parapsychologist from Duke University. He is hoping to gather scientific proof that death does not exist."

I was honored and confused. Mike's death and my life, after all, were private matters. "I need time to decide," I said.

I went to my room. After an hour, all I could decide on was the need to find a tree and meditate. So I headed downstairs to the front door. When I got to the bottom step, a voice rang out, "Go for it, Mom!" I fell on my ass.

A woman nearby looked me squarely in the eye and said, "You couldn't have a clearer answer than that!"

"You heard it, too?" I asked.

"Of course," she replied.

I wasn't nervous about the seance. In meditation, I had indicated my intention to be a channel for whoever was trying to manifest. I was calm and ready. We sat in a circle and meditated. A microphone was placed around my neck. Patricia told me to close my eyes and concentrate on a time when Mike and I were close. I focused on my thirty-third birthday party. She instructed me to repeat Mike's name aloud three times while sending out welcoming, loving energy. As people in the circle articulated impressions of my son, I was to answer yes or no, depending on whether or not they were accurate. I kept my eyes closed so I could concentrate without being distracted by the television cameras.

A woman said she saw a tall boy with curly brown hair and a half-shut left eye.

"Yes," I said. (Mike had a lazy eye muscle when he was born.)

Another woman said Mike was telling her about his broken wrist.

"Yes," I said. (Two months before he died, he broke his wrist.)

"I see a picture of three boys in a boat, and the word *newspaper*," said a third participant.

"Yes!" I exclaimed. (A week before Mike died, he and two friends took a boat into a flooded street, then a staff photographer came and captured the scene for the local paper.)

Someone else spoke up, saying Mike was showing her a large rock-bound coastline with two watchtowers.

"Yes," I said tearfully, "that's Two Lights, where we enjoyed family picnics, and where I later scattered Mike's ashes."

Someone asked if the name "Auntie Bee" meant anything to me.

"No," I said.

"Are you sure?" she persisted. "Mike wants Auntie Bee to know he is all right. He wants to see Auntie Bee free. It's very important to him."

"No," I said. "I don't understand."

"He is showing me a silver and turquoise ring, and he wants you to know the ring will be returned to you within four days, in a most unusual way."

Tears streamed down my face. Mike had given me a silver and turquoise ring on my thirty-third birthday. I searched for it after he died, but never found it.

"You will be a believer soon—within four days. Hold the ring tightly, because it will have his vibrations," someone else counseled me.

One woman started to cry and said, "I love you, Mom. I love you, Mom. I love you, Mom. I had to leave. I am a healer. And you must believe me before you can receive the healing love I bring to you."

"But did you have to *die,* Mike?" I asked out loud.

"I did what was necessary. And I bring the gift of healing to you. Tell my sister, 'Mikey is okay.'"

"She knows." I then asked what I had to do to receive more fully.

"Mom, there is one more release. You have not let yourself go yet. You will know when you have, and I will send you a sign of completion. I will be with you."

The room was alive with light, with love.

A woman said, "He holds a pen and paper, and he will be with you as you write. Healing for others comes through your pen. Together you are a team." I sighed.

The group sent love to Mike and to all others in the spirit dimension. Then the lights dimmed, and people began to move about. I was sitting still, certain that the questions had run their course, when someone came up and asked me who Mike was with when he died.

"His friend Artie B.," I replied. Suddenly I began laughing and crying, one after the other, for I realized that the "Auntie Bee" referred to earlier was Mike's best friend, Artie B.

Someone suggested that we dance. Another person lit candles, and six of us began shadow-dancing in pairs, slowly following the movements of our partners. *Snap!* This was precisely the release Mike had hinted at. Instantly, a blinding light beamed from the mantelpiece over the fireplace. One of the dancers said in a hushed voice, "There's your sign, Rosie."

For six years, I had held myself back from dancing with a partner. I had abandoned my inner rhythms, my link to eternity. With my heart opened, I danced till I could dance no more. As I moved, memories came rushing back at me: I saw the mysterious dancing partner of my dreams, scenes of playfully dancing with Mike's spirit during the acid trip, even my solo dance at the friary. All coalesced, and I felt the vastness of this script called life.

I vowed to myself, to Mike, and to other energies who may have been present that I would do whatever was needed to spread the healing message that the survival connection does exist, that energy is simply information and is forever available.

April 13, 1983

*F*eeling a sense of reverence, I breathe in love from the universe and announce my readiness to channel.

I came to see in clouds of white light. I am your son, and I join you in radiance, which for you is experienced as revelations. I smile, and we dance.

Draw close to me, for I whisper inspiration on all levels. In quietness, I come to you. In joy, I come. Be alive and I breathe more life into you.

Allow me to magnetize our energy. It is a great field in which we attract all that resonates with the joy of the universe. Join the dance. Be one with the music and the movement. Grant yourself permission to be filled with joy, for joy is the energy which gives me the light to channel through you.

Embrace your essence, which is pure attraction for revelry. Sometimes revelry is quiet; other times it is energetic. Always revelry is moving toward revelation. Never confuse revelry with hectic ways. Revelry is pure magnetized energy, free of static. Release from your soul all particles that do not attract golden energy. You have agreed to express the fullness of who you are—you are music and dance, poetry and movement. Be free to offer unto others what you know to be the genuine truth of living and loving.

Truths are simple. Be receptive and know your own truths. Smile, laugh, cry, and embrace eternity, for I am with you in all ways. Draw close unto yourself and we are one.

I take a long inhalation, unaware until that I have not been breathing. Do I dare believe that Mike has been my prompter, feeding me information behind the scenes for the last six years? I giggle.

How simple it all is. I have no choice but to continue receiving direction, "revelations," and love.

April 14, 1983

*W*hen I returned from the workshop, Kelli-Lynne greeted me by dashing out of my mother's car, twirling around me, and telling me to close my eyes and hold out my hand because she had a surprise for me. Caught up in her excitement, I did as I was told, whereupon she dropped a small, smooth object into my palm. I knew it was the turquoise ring. I opened my eyes, smiled in delight, and danced with my daughter.

"I found it at Grandmom's—at the bottom of her jewelry box. And I knew it really belonged to you, so I brought it home so you can wear it and remember Mikey," she said gleefully.

I bent down to kiss her, but she darted off to play with friends.

"Thank you," I said, looking from Kelli-Lynne to the sun. "Thank you." I felt light, a little embarrassed that I needed evidence, and delighted that my daughter was included in the return of the ring. We remain a family! Six anguishing years after Mike's death, we are connected in love.

I walked inside and settled down with my journal. Instantly words flowed through my pen, filling two blank pages.

You are surrounded by love in all realms. Trust love to be as limitless as consciousness. Let your mind expand, and know that we are "reality at your command." Our job is to perfect your clairaudience and clairsentience so that you can be a direct link between worlds.

Set aside time daily. That's right—the pang you felt in your throat is a sign that we will be speaking through you. You will be communicating from trance. Soaring will become familiar to you; trust that you will be able to handle the heights in a gentle, humorous, and unique way.

You will be called upon to translate messages from other dimensions. There is no chance that you will lose your way or become inflated with admiration from others.

∞ ∞

Your path is set. We have been beckoning for a long time. Your first mission is to compile the reports of instances in which we were present for you and you were absent to the fullness that surrounded you. May our many blessings magnify your heart. It is indeed a pleasure to have you so present. Good day.

I am tickled to know I can consciously access information. For the moment, I have no need to know how it comes to me or who is in charge. All I know is that I will do my part.

Dance is centering and is part of your own healing process. Just as there is a time for relaxing meditation, so is there a time for more active release. Allow your movements to free you. Dance as if your every step is filling the room with fresh, welcoming energy—for indeed, that is what you are doing. Dance with grace. Dance in abandonment. Dance with no thoughts, only the delight of dancing. Dance will become precious to you.

Trust the pauses. Know that truth appears during these recesses. Welcome each pause as you would a recess. Know, too, that wisdom often resides in silence. By allowing your mind to rest, you enter into receptivity. Relish the pleasure of "no mind." The mystery requires your receptive cooperation. Without the pause, there is no room.

April 20, 1983

Instead of asking a direct question, I simply breathe deeply and fully, and ask for information that is important to know right now. Without a second's interruption, my pen begins to move.

Yes, you are indeed getting your house in order—cleaning up, dusting off, throwing out, ordering. In all ways, energy manifests. The cleaning and clearing you are doing in your house is an outward expression of your inner activity. One reflects the other. There is no division, for inner and outer are one. Divisions are a dimension of the physical level in which you reside. Unity is the natural way.

April 26, 1983

While attempting to engage in a dialogue with whoever or whatever is in charge of the information coming my way, I write: "What are the most important concepts I need to remember about becoming a translator?"

Know that energy is a dance—the dance of life, the dance of simplest forms. Trust yourself to respond with grace to the truths of life, which are essentially the truths of light. Never force a dance. A dance is an expression of the impression.

Nothing is ever static. Just as the moving wave curls in upon itself, you must also bend in to yourself.

Refinement is important to you. As you are already aware, while you sleep, we assist in your physical refinements—that is, your body is being worked on while you rest. In your sleep you have been receiving instruction, traveling, talking to others, but most importantly, practicing the skills that are becoming yours. Dreams are opportunities for watching yourself without judgment and interference.

Notice the signs that indicate we are with you. We reassure you of our presence through subtle signs—like right now, the soft touch on your left cheek. When you were an infant, gross signals were necessary; now that you are more conscious, subtle are the signs.

Develop discipline. Each day spend some time writing or drawing. Invite us in. Begin by meditating or dancing. We, too, need signs that you are ready to continue your work. Prepare yourself by becoming relaxed in an uncluttered environment.

Ready yourself to be awakened, for you have opened yourself up and invited us in, saying, "Use me. Use me. Use me." And that is our intention.

Be patient. Be receptive. Be with love in all you do. Adopt a loving attitude in living, for only through love are you receptive. Go with love.

Feeling pushed to reveal Mike's story and my subsequent experiences, I posed my next question: "How do I begin telling this story?"

Own your power. Own your gifts. You have earned the right to be instrumental in educating people about the continuing existence of energy. People will tell you their stories, and you will collect more accounts of the survival connection. You inspire questions of a very deep and delicate nature by telling your story. Some will not want to listen; that is their way. Do not allow questions or criticism to deter you.

You will not be able to answer the question of why death interrupts the life of a loved one, but you can educate people to become sensitive instruments. As channels, they will still grieve and there will be great pain, yet they will be able to form a living connection with the one who has passed into spirit. Once the connection is made on a conscious level, comfort and gentling will come. There is an enormous need for parents who have survived the death of a child to tell their stories, write of their experiences, and talk about the unseen connections they feel.

Thinking our "conversation" had come to a close, I suddenly felt a familiar energy surge through me. Then more words appeared.

I do not want my story kept private. I am working with you to further beliefs of an evidential nature about the existence of energy after death. Together we are joined in that goal. You brought life to me, and I bring to you news of continuing life. Go in peace and love.

The "I" was Mike! A flush of recognition informed me that he was indeed behind the blink-truths that for years had been filling the pages of my journals. Knowing that Mike is behind the scenes, I am prepared to proceed with trust and courage.

April 29, 1983

It is late afternoon when I sit down with my journal. In a contemplative frame of mind, I begin wondering if I have in fact been receiving information from "the other side" these six years.

That's right. You have been picking up transmissions for many years. As you review your past journals you will become more appreciative of your receptivity. At times your faith has faltered, yet you have made the decision to become whole. Your attention has shifted from surviving to healing. Sorrow exists. Healing exists. Only by embracing pain were you able to be present for healing. The time has come for you to publicly acknowledge the work you have been engaged in privately since your son died. Your credentials are noteworthy because you are both a survivor and a healer.

Many parents experience the pain that accompanies the death of a child, for a child is anyone born to another, regardless of how long that individual has lived. Many people need evidence that love and growth are not extinguished at physical death, that evolution continues eternally.

Let there be no mistake about it: grief is essential when a loved one dies, because that person ceases to exist in physical form. Yet, a greater connection can be activated in time. The belief that all life is lost at death severs the link between parent and child. An openness to the existence of energy after death allows us inspirited ones to send messages to you who have chosen to live on the earth plane.

In ways still unknown to you, relating to the inspirited one as "my son" or "my daughter" hinders communication. Too much emotion short-circuits the transmission between dimensions. We who have recently been transported to spirit become charged by emotional links, for we are students, not masters.

Initially, static exists on both sides. Grief holds all in bondage. Here we inspirited ones are known not as sons or daughters, but as energy vibrating and resonating at specific frequencies. Bondage to past relationships would offer survivors only reassurance, not direction. The purpose of the energy transmission, on the other hand, is to offer direction to you who have chosen to continue in the physical dimension.

Grieve first. In the midst of grief, believe that life is infinite. Forms change. Energy transcends. Only when grief subsides can the energy transmission begin with any clarity that rings of truth for the survivor. Before the acceptance of the physical death, there exist sentimental wonderings. Without clarity of both heart and mind, insights are dismissed as simple longings.

Many on your side do not talk about their dreams of us or their experiences with us, for fear of being ridiculed. As more people begin to share what cannot be explained by logic, others will gather the courage to tell of their experiences, and human consciousness will grow.

Know and appreciate the difference between possessive love and love that promotes wholeness. The love of mother for child is possessive and becomes ever more possessive as death intervenes. In contrast, unified love recognizes essence, and in essence we are all one.

We of this dimension attract people in your dimension who resonate with the vibration of love. We work with you. We also work for you, because our growth and evolution depend on your continued evolution. Through you, we work to activate higher consciousness—or, to use your words, an awareness of "multidimensional realities." Through you, we can bring about so-called miracles. We manifest in order to enhance the recognition of truths in your dimension.

I go downstairs to fix supper, like millions of people do each day, yet I am infused with a sense of purpose and destiny. After supper I return to the typewriter, realizing how important it is to conduct my life as an ordinary woman and also as a receptive channel.

Make neither reality more important than the other, for balance is crucial. Go about your daily work: clean your house, water your plants, spend time with friends, make love, and be receptive to our energies. Never renounce the ordinary for the extraordinary. Open to us in your fullness, and bring your fullness to those you cherish, knowing that the love vibration is the energy that connects, transcends, and makes miracles possible.

I am in awe of this entire production—its timing and plot, the characters, the themes, even my nighttime dreams. It appears that guides have been giving me cues for some time and my part has been to record the evolving story, to serve as a cosmic secretary duly noting the connection that exists between the dimensions we call life and death. Reciprocity has been the governing principle—as it is in birthing.

May 1, 1983

By knowing I am growing, I am growing in knowing. I have no questions. I am ready for dictation.

The importance of grief cannot be overlooked, for in the grieving is the release—the letting go of the relationship that existed in your dimension. Energy, you must remember, is vast. When we visit or communicate with you, we present ourselves as you remember us. Otherwise, we might not capture your attention. For, as you shall see, dear lady, this work involves the energy of many. It is not sufficient that we, the inspirited ones, assist you. You, the survivors, also have a commitment.

Many have been awaiting the opportunity to work with you. Your son, Mike, captured your attention and is to be congratulated. Be not overly invested in connecting only with the energy field of your son, however, for he has much to learn. Know that by agreeing to record the energies of many, you evolve and your son also evolves.

Our realm is peopled with spirits who specialize in different forms of training. I, O-Lan, attend to the adepts on earth, those who have clearly committed to being channels of light and intelligence. I have long been aware of you. I have encouraged you through your writing, ever awaiting the time to announce myself. Each affirmation you made to become a healing channel has consecrated our connection. The pain you experienced in your forehead was my attempt to modulate our energies. Such refinements are needed so you can both receive and question. Believe in the reality of the words you are typing. Trust in the healing you have already accomplished. Have faith in your dreams. Adhere to this guidance and your work will continue to create light-fullness for yourself and others.

While reading these words, I shake my head in amazement. Other than the guide who has identified herself by name, I have no idea who the "we" is behind the channeling, and at this moment I have no need to know. Furthermore, I have no idea where I am headed and, for the record, no fear of losing or sacrificing something that is precious to me.

Trust is present within my mind, heart, and soul.

May 2, 1983

As tired as I was when I got home from work, I fixed supper for Kelli-Lynne and read her a story before tucking her in bed. Then I poured a glass of wine and started to read through years of journal entries.

I am not the same woman who grieved Mike's death six years ago. I feel less attached to missing his earthly antics and more connected to his essence. His birthday, two days away, seems like an occasion for celebrating our deliverance from bondage to ordinary consciousness. Living in a multidimensional reality is very simple: growth awaits while love underlies and unites all.

May 4, 1983

Happy day of your earthly birth, Mike. Because of you I became a mother for the first time. Quietness and awe have replaced that unsettled feeling I've had since your death. When I open to receive the universal energies, we are one. All I have to do is be receptive, honest, trusting, and loving. Thank you for your love and for your ongoing participation in my life.

May 5, 1983

Appreciate the gardenia and the three roses you have placed on the desk in front of you, for they bring you the fragrance of life. It is no coincidence that the gardenia you bought for yourself at Christmas burst forth in blossom on the anniversary of your son's birth—another sign that you are being nurtured on all levels. Go in peace, love, and joy.

May 8, 1983

Notice the energy you expend while berating yourself. Be free to learn as you are working in a new dimension. Understanding will come. You weigh yourself down by persistently thinking you should already know things. Still your mind, for we have much to transmit to you. Understanding will come if you simply write.

Letting go of thinking is hard to do. I've always tried to make sense of events. I am noticing a different energy now. Is someone here?

Yes, very good. I am here to swiftly pass on information to you. I work with children and want you to know that the way to insight is the way of the child. For now, it is necessary to fill yourself with the spirit of play, inquisitiveness, and spontaneity. Get to know your child within. Become more childlike. Visit the outdoors. Crouch down, and make yourself smaller so you will experience the vastness of life. Know that the world is home to a child.

May 10, 1983

You invite as you write. Be aware that when you chose to work with spirit, you committed to connect with the energy in order to translate the information. Resistance is a sign that you are struggling with your limited personality.

As you grow more fully within the light, you will fuse with all that is, and you will acquire the ability to consistently access the power and gentleness of love-wisdom. The echoes of eternity resonate within your soul. Doubt not yourself or our intervention when the work is not gliding easily. You have devoted much effort to keeping this record of your journey, so partake of the feast. Go in peace and beauty.

While reading my notebooks, I have indeed been feeling a sense of contentment. The dreams I have recorded are like transmissions that have been received, and I know there are others just waiting to be intercepted. In many ways, this adventure is like a giant game of cosmic catch!

Mother's Day 1983

Mother's Day was a rare treat free of jagged edges. I awoke early and read more journals. On the radio, I heard the dj announce that in honor of both the Greek Orthodox Easter and Mother's Day, he would play George Frideric Handel's Messiah. Turning up the volume, I continued reading, all the while feeling close to Mike and hoping the chorus would come fast and add to my joy.

Beyond intimacy is infinity.

May 14, 1983

Continue to be aware. Note the opportunities and challenges that accompany a multidimensional perspective. Also pay attention to how a family adjusts and grows within this expanded system. Your relationships with your living family members are as important as your relationship with your son. Remember that your life is an overlay designed to alert you to the existence of parallel realities.

May 18, 1983

I am accepting the seriousness of retrieval times. Even spirit waited patiently as I reread my journals. Perhaps all along, spirit has been my coauthor!

May 19, 1983

Last night I had a vivid dream about Mike and me. I was driving a large green van to the local Holiday Inn, and Mike was sitting beside me. We were about to round a corner when I noticed that he, too, had a steering wheel. In fact, he was the one driving the van even though he was in the passenger's seat! I laughed—how preposterous that all this time I

had been thinking I was the one in control! I relaxed and let him negotiate the curves.

While napping in the late afternoon, I was aware of receiving truths
essential to hold in my mind.

May 25, 1983

*T*here are many artists within you.

This unsolicited message brings a sense of renewal. I am not forgotten, even though I have not been working on my channeling. Life is not
a test after all!

June 3, 1983

A women's healing ritual workshop I designed is scheduled to take
place tomorrow. I have prepared an outline and an hour-long tape of
songs cut from my favorite women's music. I plan to create an environment in which we can reconnect with ourselves as women of vision,
women of wonder, women of wisdom. Then I will invite all participants
to extend beyond their wounds and lost innocence. My hope is that we
will expand enough to integrate our visions into our daily lives despite
the hardships we are grappling with.

Music and color, dance and symbols will be our tools. Beyond these,
I am relying on our capacity as women to be spontaneous ritual-makers.
Our intuitions will lead the way.

This evening I checked in for any additional information my guides
might have. I asked: "What's important for me to know about tomorrow's
workshop?"

*Know that you have prepared well. Know, too, that the women are
ready. Clarity, along with a deepened sense of the significance of rituals, is
manifesting for all participants. They will be thirsty and eager to drink
deeply from their own fountains.*

*You, dear one, are a catalyst. You are both guide and learner, and you
create a pregnant environment in which birthings occur. Publicly be the
channel that you are. Encourage all to reconnect with their own intuitive
wisdom, for that is the fount from which all rituals arise. Be with reverence.
Be in fullness. Invite each woman to embrace her fullness.*

June 7, 1983

The ritual workshop was thrilling. For the first time ever, I called myself a channel in public. And there was another first: for most of the two-day event, I simply *let* it happen, which is nothing like trying to *make* it happen. Instinctively, I knew what was needed, and I trusted the women to voice their needs, fears, and wisdom.

On day one, someone asked the group, "When was the first time you realized you were a woman?" Stories flowed. We spoke of wounds sustained in attempting to declare our femininity. Rapes, incest, divorces, hysterectomies, lost loves, abortions, and deaths were common. Music and movement facilitated our expression of grief and its release. Into the void we descended, bearing silk scarves, incense, feather boas, peacock feathers, music, crystals and candles, robes, yarn, paint, and our journals.

I proved to be a perfected instrument of timing. Before each session, I would cloister myself in a room and dedicate myself to being a channel for healing energy; then I'd wait. Returning to the group, I could feel energy flow through me. I invited others to dip into their intuitive wisdom and move with it. Evidently it is possible to be a midwife to energy.

Setting the principles of love and light to paper is easy; living them is a challenge. And yet, philosophizing is not enough for me—I must participate in living, loving, laughing, and lighting. This is my lifework, the elusive "direction" I have been seeking.

As the first day of the workshop drew to a close, I breathed a sigh of relief. Then in the evening, I gave a soul reading for a friend, and in the course of the reading I went into trance. I was frightened to hear my voice while feeling far away from my body, and I was terrified of going too deeply into a trance state. Suddenly I saw an image of a woman being hanged for misusing her powers. Something I must have viewed on television when I was a kid, I figured.

The following day, a woman named Armada asked if I would barter a soul reading for a massage, and I agreed. During the massage, Armada asked if I had ever broken my neck. "No," I replied emphatically, but I began to tremble. Immediately I was struck by the chilling realization that the hanged woman was *me,* and that I had been executed for the misuse of power in a previous lifetime. No wonder I have been afraid of my power, I thought to myself.

Two large black snakes appeared at my neck during the integration part of the massage. At first I was afraid.

As long as you invest in love, you have nothing to fear.

The two snakes collared my neck.

When you do trance work, remember the serpents. And know you are protected.

I watched the snakes slither down my body, encircle my feet, and move up to my neck once again. No longer afraid, I affirmed the loving use of my psychic abilities. Channel I must, I asserted, even if it requires trance work.

While doing the soul reading for Armada, I remained in a trance for an hour and a half. The experience was so profound that I decided to come to terms with my fear. I simply cannot afford to be in my own way, I told myself.

The use of power is one of your life lessons. In your attempts to be absolutely certain that you do not misuse power, you have neglected to appreciate that you are not being true to your essence; when you bow to the fear of misusing power, you do not allow power in. Your ability and ambition to be a channel for the loving light is outstanding. Trance work makes the fullest use of the available energy by creating a more direct circuit. Think of it as an energy-efficient form of healing.

Yes, you have misused power in the past by utilizing psychic energy for your own selfish ends. And yes, your neck was broken in a most violent manner. There is no need in this life to have your neck or your spirit broken. You have learned the lessons well. You know you are a vehicle, not the light itself.

With consistency, you are receiving and expressing inspiration. You are allowing yourself to become illuminated, and you are beckoning others toward enlightenment. People respond to your insights.

It is curious to think that not utilizing my psychic gifts constitutes a misuse of energy.

June 18, 1983

On the plane to Buffalo for another week at CPSI, I asked for any information that might assist me during my time there.

Be relaxed. Drink in refreshment on all levels. Eat lightly; remember that liquor is not light. Invite the Genesa crystal concepts you are about to encounter to seep gradually into your body and into your inner being. Genesa movements encourage revelations and insights to merge. In the process, molecular memory becomes activated.

Remember that you are a generalist and you need a model that has general applications. Honor the freedom to transform. Discipline yourself to learn the basics before suggesting other dimensions. Be sure to document the steps forward and backward, for the source is ever the same. Go in peace. Be grateful for the blessings of eternity which rest within your heart.

I arrived at the institute feeling renewed. Rather than attending the opening session, I went to sit alone on "my mountain" and ask for guidance.

Part of the responsibility of being a healer is to be finely attuned to the sources of healing. Free yourself from all that interferes with clarity. Wisdom awaits. Discriminate. Be polite to yourself. Honor the urge to create a cocoon for yourself. Replenish your energies in this cocoon.

The next initiation requires you to be still. Know that when you are freely present you invite spiritual energies to empower you, and you also encourage others to join in.

The large, walk-in Genesa crystals were made of plexiglass pipes developed by plant geneticist Derald Langham. They were designed to represent the body's cellular energy fields. Specific movements within this environment, we were told, would help the body relate to nature's principles of harmony, balance, rhythm, and symmetry, while awakening body memories of instinct, intuition, insight, and inspiration. [See For More Information on page 197.]

The workshop leader, Kay Bruch, began by introducing us to movements that replicated cellular division. Following her motions while listening to Deuter's "Ecstasy" playing in the background, I felt my soul being prepared for something new. I closed my eyes to swirls of oranges and yellows. Within minutes I saw an image of Mike sitting in a wicker chair, his hands forming the shape of a diamond. The image circled me to the left and the right, creating an infinity sign. I then danced with the energy of infinity and did not cease until the music stopped. Breathing in the familiar presence of Mike, I drew large orange and yellow infinity signs on a blank piece of paper, and below them, with an orange crayon, I wrote the following lines:

I am timeless.
I touch you with eternity.
I bow. We dance.
Together, we glide to the rhythms of universal energy.
As you reinvest, we move with universal rhythms,
One with love, one with beauty, one with light.

The energy dance has begun, and the dance is filled with revelations for you. Prepare to embody naturalness, for that is the gift of eternity.

Tears of reverence slipped down my cheeks, puddling my picture-poem.

After a break, Kay put on "Ecstasy" again. This time she invited us to use the Genesa movements on our own. Pulsing, waving, and spiraling, I moved with abandon until the dance danced me. When the music stopped, I sank to my knees and rested in the stillness that the experience had created within me. In this spiraling silence, I became aware of another familiar presence—not Mike this time, but God.

I lay on my back with arms outstretched and heart wide open, letting the God-presence fill me. I knew for the first time in my life that I was deserving of blessings. All that existed was the mystery!

Back on the hill, journal in hand, I contemplated the limitless impulses stirring within me.

Yes, another initiation for you. God is with you. You are beaming with vibrations of the divine. Embrace your own divinity. You have gained the respect of many people, and you have touched numerous hearts and souls. More readiness will bring deeper revelations. It is essential for you to acknowledge your depths. Affirm your gifts, for you are a direct channel.

June 23, 1983

Be still. Know that the silence holds all that you are. Be with your breath. Breathe the fragrance of life. Be protective of your energy, for it is all you have. It is time to more firmly establish your own rhythms. You must announce with your energy who you are. Speak from the fullness of your heart, for at the center of stillness echoes the voice of eternity. Know that you carry love in your eyes, and use them to welcome others. Aligning yourself with truth, as you are doing, you will perform from insights that are eternal. Honor the quietness. Honor the flow of energy within you. Above all, honor the moment.

July 8, 1983

"*P*lease give me some information about how to communicate my experience," I write. "I feel overwhelmed and in awe."

An infusion of light, wisdom, love, and beauty resides within you. Your cosmic evolution will be gentle, moving smoothly toward more light and revelation. Gentle, too, will be your visioning, as experiencing cosmic consciousness too abruptly can be dangerous for one with your sensitivities. The leap you experienced while embracing the living, loving source has yet to make its full impact on you.

Remember how you discovered the source. You were open to inspiration while remaining free of expectation. You beckoned with movements informed by the cosmos. You danced to universal rhythms, announcing your readiness to embrace even more. You furthered your consciousness by entering the mystery. Your mind was at peace, free of questions or ideas. This is the essence of higher initiations.

Grace and appreciation can be present in abundance. A sense of timelessness, gentle knowing, reverence, a molecular infusion of peacefulness, and a silent understanding accompany revelatory visions. You continue to associate pain, grief, and letting go with initiations. Struggle and sadness, however, are not resonant with revelation.

Remember that you can call upon my guidance at will. Know, too, that at times I will not wait for your call, but will make my presence known to you in my own way. Remember that you are blessed, you carry blessings with you, and you bestow blessings upon all you meet.

July 20, 1983

*N*or Hall, a Jungian analyst, offered a weekend workshop called Spiritual Rites of Passage for Women in Mid-Life. The moment I saw the announcement, I knew I needed to attend.

At the workshop I learned about two-thousand-year-old frescoes that were discovered in the ancient city of Pompeii in southern Italy. These frescoes depict the journey of women claimed by spirit. According to the inscriptions, Dionysus—"the loosener" for the infusion of spirit— demands of a woman on the spiritual journey to return to the instinctual. As she does, she is drawn by an irresistible call to enter the mystery.

Enveloped by the mystery, she becomes terrified, for she meets death without actually dying. Once the call is heard, there is no turning back.

The initiate quickly becomes aware of her inner emptiness. She desires to be filled from the inside out, despite her roles in life. During this portion of the journey, she passes into the underworld where, fearful of losing her soul, she falls prey to confusion and eventually depression. Dismemberment comes next, along with the promise that she will get to see all the parts of her former self. In facing death without dying, she is granted the opportunity to meet the gods and goddesses within her. She gradually surrenders to a force greater than herself and becomes an instrument of transformation.

One of the frescoes shows an angel who, with whip in hand, is coming down on a woman in the underworld. Her experience is being beaten into form as she is brought back to her senses. All the while, the woman is holding her hands over a veiled phallus. The angel warns her that it is not yet time to reveal the phallus as both sexual and sacred, that it holds intimate knowledge of a woman's body, much the same as a baby does. Forever afterward, the initiate will not be able to separate sexuality from spirituality.

In a final fresco, a priestess is combing the initiate's hair. She, meanwhile, must gaze into the mirror to see the dismembered parts of herself so that she may re-member them and, hence, depart reintegrated from the underworld. Upon completion of the cycle, the initiate returns to the world forever changed. [See For More Information on page 197.]

Although the initiation itself is a collective experience, each woman's call—and its timing—is unique. It may follow a surgical procedure, the end of a loving relationship, the death of a child, or any other soul-wresting experience. Upon dying to ourselves and what we once believed in, we cannot turn back. We can, however, return from our individual underworlds and embrace life with imagination, passion, and new purpose.

My cells have lived this journey. My hands have recorded it. My soul, long immersed in healing grief, has found its way home in love.

For More Information

Creative Education Foundation
1050 Union Road, Buffalo, NY 14224

Genesa Foundation
c/o Lisa Langham Parvel, 40702 San Jacinto Circle, Fallbrook, CA 92028

Nor Hall, *Those Women* (1988), published by:
Spring Publications, Inc.
299 East Quassett Road, Woodstock, CT 06281

About the Author

ROSALIE DEER HEART has practiced for twenty years as a psychotherapist specializing in psychospiritual integration and women's adult development. She is on the faculty of the Creative Problem Solving Institute of New York University in Buffalo, where she teaches the spiritual foundations of creativity, soul empowerment, and women's rites of passage. She is also an Interfaith Minister and coauthor of *Affectuve Education Guidebook: Classroom Activities in the Realm of Feelings* (1975) and *Affective Direction: Planning and Teaching for Thinking and Feeling* (1979).

A licensed medium, Rosie offers soul readings by phone or in person. She designs retreats, workshops, and spiritual journeys to Egypt, Bali, Pompeii, and New Mexico. In addition she is "co-femifester" of Ripe Tomato Connections, a greeting card, journal, and T-shirt company that celebrates women's transitions.

ORDERING INFORMATION

For additional copies of *Healing Grief: A Mother's Story,* please mail your order, together with your name, address, and check or money order, to:

Heart Link Publications
PO Box 273
San Cristobal, NM 87564

800-716-2953

Please enclose US $14.95 plus $2.05 postage and handling per book.
Canadian residents: CAN $21.05 plus $3.00 postage and handling per book.
United Kingdom residents: £10.16 plus £1.50 postage and handling per book.
Quantity discounts available.